How to Manage Real Estate Profitably

Andrew James McLean

Additional titles by Andrew James McLean

The Power of Real Estate
REAL ESTATE: The Ultimate Handbook
The POWER OF FINANCIAL INDEPENDENCE

Additional books of interest from Delphi:

Title	Unit Price
Numbers Guide for Real Estate (PB)	3.95
Numbers Guide for Real Estate (Spiral)	6.95
Payment Tables 8% to 14%	3.50
The Complete Payment Book	3.25
Mortgage Yield Tables (Hard cover)	20.00
Income Property Illustrated (Hard cover)	9.95
Mortgage Yield Tables (PB)	15.00
How to Grow a Moneytree	6.95
Income Property Illustrated (PB)	5.95
Real Estate Dictionary (PB)	3.95
How to Manage Real Estate Profitably (PB)	5.95
The Power of Real Estate (PB)	4.95
The Power of Financial Independence (PB)	5.95
Real Estate — The Ultimate Handbook (PB)	4.95

Send list price plus $1.10 for postage and handling (California residents please add 6% sales tax) to: *Delphi Information Sciences, 1416 6th St., Santa Monica, CA 90401.*

Andrew James McLean

How to Manage Real Estate Profitably

Newly Revised Edition 1979

Delphi Information Sciences Corporation, 1416 6th Street, Santa Monica, CA 90401

For purposes of clarity the author employed masculine pronouns instead of using "he and she" or "his and her", which is more difficult to read. Sexism is neither intended nor implied.

Published by Delphi Information Sciences Corporation, 1416 6th Street, Santa Monica, California 90401.

First Printing   1978

Second Printing   1979

Preface

Since the beginning of time, real estate has controlled the ultimate destiny of the entire world. Countries have fought tragic wars over it . . . millions have died for it . . . and most millionaires are made from it.

Real estate is the basis for a country's wealth. Its natural resources and productive facilities are derived from the land. It is my intention to show you how to effectively manage all the real estate you might ever acquire or be responsible for.

This text is a cross-section from my learning experience while successfully operating my own properties and those of my past employers. I endeavored to be thorough; to offer you a complete guide for total property management . . . assisting you at making decisions and avoiding costly pitfalls.

Essentially, it is a complete do-it-yourself guide, including do-it-yourself repairs and evictions. I have also included real estate definitions, a monthly loan payment table, and the latest in practice and forms you'll need to profitably operate residential income property.

Property management can be a wonderful experience, as it has been for me; or it can be a burdensome daily chore. It is my intention to simplify all the necessary functions you will need to know to operate effectively, efficiently, and profitably; to eventually enable you to turn over individual management responsibility of every building to a competent resident manager. You can then begin to oversee your total estate, with more leisure time to enjoy whatever you care to.

It's been a decade since I took an $11,000 inheritance, squandered it in the stock market, and six months later had a meager $5,000 remaining. That costly experience involved many a sleepless night while wrestling with a volatile market where random price movements and unforseen circumstances cause many Wall Street investors to gamble away fortunes.

Fortunately for me, I took what I had left and invested in a small home where my successful trek in real estate began, never again to have an interest in the misfortunes of Wall Street.

I hate to sound overly biased against the stock market, but the fact remains that for every winner on Wall Street, there are four losers. Real estate, however, has been a sound investment over the last fifty years, and it continues to be, mainly because demand continues strong and there is a limited supply.

Since my unfortunate experience at buying and selling stocks, I've had the opportunity to invest in various single family homes and apartment buildings that all began with that one moderate "fixer-upper" which allowed me a base to reinvest from.

While I continued to dabble, investing in real estate part time, my full time occupation was that of a property manager for a shrewd family who owned in excess of one hundred commercial properties located in Michigan. Later in California, I managed 363 residential units for a large real estate developer who operated 16,000 units throughout the country. From there, my career led me to managing six million dollars in foreclosure property for a major savings and loan association, and to real estate appraisal.

From this experience I have contrived all the necessary guidelines to assist anyone in managing residential income property.

If you own or manage, or plan to own or manage any form of residential real estate, this book was written and dedicated to you.

ANDREW JAMES McLEAN

How to Manage
Real Estate
Profitably

Contents

You Versus Property Management Firm

Professional property management companies usually charge from 5% to 10% of gross collected rents for their services. This fee varies with the size and character of each particular property. Management responsibilities are to operate the building, paying all expenses, and send the owner a report of their activities along with a monthly check for proceeds, if any.

Like any other business, property management firms have their share of professionals and incompetents; but for the most part, they earn their fees. The incompetent companies not only operate very inefficiently, in doing so they cheat the owners of deserving profits.

Besides having the inability to operate efficiently, incompetent management firms can cheat unsuspecting owners in various, unscrupulous ways. Just to mention a few of the schemes, I have listed some methods that occur frequently to naive owners: property managers billing unsuspecting owners for expenses that do not exist; renting a vacant apartment and continuing to declare to the owner that the unit is still vacant; charging owners more than a reasonable amount for painting and repair work. Besides these common methods of cheating by shady managers, there are other more involved schemes; some that haven't even been dreamed up yet.

Just being aware of how you can be cheated is a form of defense in itself. You should always be somewhat suspicious of new people you do business with.

Turning the management responsibility over to a professional firm would obviously cost you five to ten percent of gross collected rents of each building you own. Assuming your total holdings are sixty units, consisting of varying sizes of buildings, then your gross collectable rent would be in the neighborhood of $180,000 per year. (60 units × $250 per month rent × 12 months equals $180,000 per year gross rent.) At a ten percent management rate, you would pay out a whopping $18,000 per year in management fees. At five percent you would only pay out $9,000 per year in fees. At either rate, I'm sure you'd agree that it would be a substantial savings to put in your pocket, not in someone else's. Besides, you'll have the incentive to operate your own estate more efficiently than a management firm.

Decisions

In this chapter, I intend to guide you in making some major decisions which you will later have to live with. The best way I know to accomplish this is to give you benefits and disadvantages of both sides of that particular decision, then let you decide for yourself.

FURNISHED VS. UNFURNISHED UNITS

Throughout the United States there has been a trend towards unfurnished units. Less turnover among tenants is the biggest advantage of unfurnished units because it requires more effort by the tenant to move in and out. Furthermore, if you, the owner, supply the furniture, it is your responsibility to maintain it. Rented units with furniture also require more expense.

On the other hand, if you own units which have single or studio apartments, it may be difficult to rent these types of units without furniture. Single and studio apartments thrive on active, transient tenants. They usually require furnishings before they move in.

APPLIANCES

Appliances such as stoves, refrigerators, and air conditioners are extremely expensive to maintain. For lower income units, I have found it advantageous *not* to supply any of these appliances whatsoever. This is somewhat typical, as you will find most lower income families are accustomed to supplying their own stoves and refrigerators. Better quality apartments usually require more appliances. If this is the case in your units, be sure it is reflected in your rental rate and the amount of deposit you require.

UTILITIES AND TRASH

In most apartment buildings, especially new models, separate meters for gas and electricity consumption are used with each apartment; the respective companies bill the individual tenants. The owner of the building is responsible for paying the water bill. When separate meters are not available for gas and electricity, the owner must add the cost to the rent and hope that the tenants are efficient with their use of energy. If you plan to own a building which lacks separate meters for each unit, consider making the change to separate meters. You'll be better off in the long run.

Trash removal is best handled by the owner. It is necessary to maintain a clean building and the only way to avoid friction among the tenants as to whose responsibility it is, is to maintain the control yourself.

LAUNDRY

What about a laundry facility? Should you buy or lease equipment? In most cases, especially with eight units or less, it may be wiser not to have machines at all. In smaller buildings, your washer and dryer would not be used enough to pay for the utility expenses.

My personal experience with laundry machines has been very good. I have two washers and two dryers in a 19-unit family building. The gross monthly receipts are between $150 and

$200 per month. Of this, the leasing company keeps 60% and sends me a check for the remaining 40% or $60 to $80. The leasing company is responsible for maintaining the equipment and the collection of the coins; the owner is responsible for paying the utilities.

Usually, with eight units or more, washers and dryers can be bought outright and pay for themselves within one to two years. Of course, you must maintain the equipment and be responsible for any acts of vandalism or theft.

If you decide to lease laundry equipment, be sure to have your resident manager oversee the removal of coins from the machines when the collection man makes his rounds. This will eliminate the temptation for him to "pocket" some of your income. Of course, if the manager and the leasing rep are in cahoots, there is little you can do.

CARPETING

Wall-to-wall carpeting will undoubtedly add a glow of warmth and value to your units. However, before you go overboard, you must consider the expense compared to the return in rental income. Instead of wall-to-wall coverage, you can keep carpeting to a minimum by using linoleum in the entrance and hallways, and even dining areas. Linoleum will last longer than carpet and save plenty of money.

When you do purchase carpeting, use a gold tweed shag of good quality. Gold tweed matches almost any furnishing color and doesn't show stains as much as other colors. Shag carpeting has the advantage over other types by being easier to patch.

The carpeting industry is very competitive, with plenty of suppliers. Therefore, it is best to shop around and get your best price. Many installers moonlight and can lay carpet for less than a package deal from a large distributor.

REDUCING TENANT TURNOVER

In order to maintain a maximum income level throughout the operation of your buildings, it will be necessary to keep vacancy loss at a minimum. By adequately maintaining your units, keeping your existing tenants satisfied within reason, you can reduce their desires to move elsewhere.

Obviously, you cannot do much about keeping a good-paying tenant under your roof when his employer requests him to relocate to another city, but you can keep good tenants by properly preserving your buildings. It begins by being reasonable about your tenant complaints and requests.

It is the landlord's responsibility to keep everything in working order; at the same time the tenant is responsible for not misusing the property he is renting. Painting, carpet shampooing, and plumbing stoppages are the owner's responsibility, but only when the tenant has given reasonable care. When a tenant continually pours grease down the kitchen drain, causing repeated stoppages, the tenant becomes responsible for the cost of repair instead of the owner.

About a year after a tenant originally moves in is usually when most maintenance or refurbishment is requested, assuming the unit was in tip-top shape initially. A wall or two may need paint, or new carpeting is needed, or maybe only a carpet shampoo is requested. It is at this point that you can lose a good tenant if you do not reasonably take care of his needs.

If your tenant moves out because you wouldn't paint a kitchen for him, it will cost you much, much more than a meager paint job. Should he move to another apartment, you not only have to prepare the unit for a new tenant, you will probably experience a vacancy loss. Therefore, instead of spending $35 for a kitchen paint job, you could lose more by spending needless money re-renting the apartment. Refurbishing the unit for a new tenant could cost $150 or more by the time you entirely repaint, clean up, shampoo the carpets, and advertise, plus the possibility of rent loss from the vacancy.

It is essential to your total operation to preserve your investment. By doing so, you will not only keep your tenants content, your vacancy loss will be kept to a minimum, allowing gross income to be at its maximum. Then your building will retain its maximum value until it is eventually sold.

Do-It-Yourself Repairs

Real estate profits can be increased substantially by the clever owner who does his own repairs. Remember, however, that an owner who does slipshod repairs on his own property can suffer unnecessary losses when one repair job has to be done three times to correct the problem.

Being a landlord is somewhat of a community responsibility; one must supply adequate accommodations to the public. A new owner may not have the working capital to do everything he would like; therefore, he needs to be flexible.

For those of you owners who would rather have someone else do all the handiwork, your best bet is to utilize the husband of your resident manager as your handyman. If, on the other hand, you plan to do your own repair work, the following material should be very useful.

Whether you do it yourself or hire the work out, you will still be responsible for the cost of supplies. Repair supplies can usually be acquired at substantial discounts; for example, you can check Sears and Roebuck for a good buy in laundry machines. It may be more feasible to rent equipment, rather than buy it.

Associate yourself with various apartment owners' organizations. They can be an excellent source of where to buy supplies and forms, and the latest laws of which you must be aware.

MAINTENANCE AND REPAIR HINTS

Some of the most common problems associated with owning multi-unit buildings are roof leaks, all types of pesky insects, broken windows, and stopped-up plumbing. The following hints are general in concept — the material that follows will describe repair work in more detail.

Broken windows are best done by a window repairman, but until he arrives, a good temporary repair is required. "See-through" contact paper may be used temporarily to protect the interior.

Plexiglass is excellent for any window that breaks frequently.

In stripping wallpaper, see your local wallpaper store for the proper removal solution.

Painting requires quality equipment. Stick with standard water-soluble paint. All enamel is to be one color; all walls are one color.

Paint with a roller using a five gallon bucket instead of a tray. Use a 12' by 15' drop cloth to protect the floor.

Cracks and holes are best filled in with Spackling compound, as are interior roof leaks.

For roaches, use powdery boric acid. D-con and peanut butter is best for mice and rats. Be careful of your pets when using these compounds.

As an owner, it is wise to look like a handyman when you approach your property, rather than a chauffeur-driven Rockefeller, because you're trying to appear like a hard-working guy, not a high-rolling big shot. You'll find that being more discreet will get you your rents faster and avoid tenants' petty complaints.

REPLACING A BROKEN WINDOW

The following information and materials are needed: Correct size of window glass, putty or a glazing compound, putty knife, hammer, pliers, and glazier points.

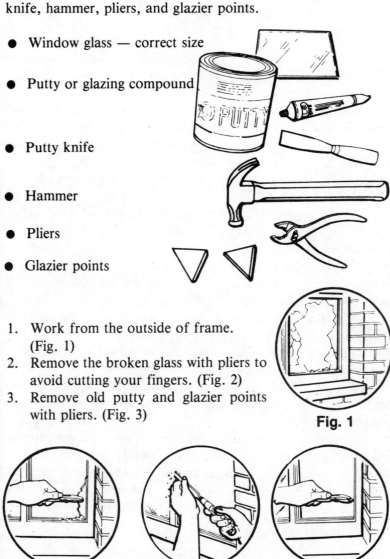

- Window glass — correct size

- Putty or glazing compound

- Putty knife

- Hammer

- Pliers

- Glazier points

1. Work from the outside of frame. (Fig. 1)
2. Remove the broken glass with pliers to avoid cutting your fingers. (Fig. 2)
3. Remove old putty and glazier points with pliers. (Fig. 3)

Fig. 1

Fig. 2   **Fig. 3**

4. Place a thin ribbon of putty in the frame. (Fig. 4)

Fig. 4

5. Place the glass firmly against the putty. (Fig. 5)

Fig. 5

6. Insert the glazier points. Tap in carefully to prevent breakage. First, place points near the corners, then every 4 to 6 inches along the glass. (Fig. 6)

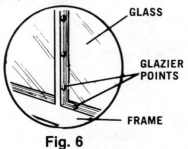

GLASS

GLAZIER POINTS

FRAME

Fig. 6

7. Fill the groove with putty or glazing compound. Press it firmly against the glass with putty knife or fingers. Smooth the surface with the putty knife. The putty should form a smooth seal around the window.

PATCH HOLES IN WALLBOARD OR PLASTER

You will need one of two types of patching compounds. Spackling compound is convenient for small jobs, but it is expensive. It can be bought as a powder, ready mixed. Patching plaster can be bought in larger packages and is better for larger jobs. You will need one of the compounds, a putty knife, medium grit sandpaper, and an old cloth or paint brush.

1. Remove any loose plaster. With a knife, scrape out plaster from back edges of the crack until the back of the crack is wider than the front surface. (Fig. 1)

Fig. 1

2. Thoroughly dampen the surface of the crack with a wet cloth or paint brush. (Fig. 2)

3. Prepare patching compound according to the directions on the package. Begin by mixing only a small amount. (Fig. 3)

Fig. 2

4. You can fill small holes with the patching mixture. Be sure to press the mixture until it completely fills the hole. Smooth the surface with putty knife. (Fig. 4) When the patch has dried, you can sand it. Wrap the sandpaper around a small piece of wood and be sure the surface is even. (Fig. 5)

Fig. 3

Fig. 4

Fig. 5

5. Larger holes or cracks should be filled step-by-step. First, partly fill the hole; let this patch dry. A base is now set for the final fill. Add a second batch of the compound and let it dry. Sand until smooth. (Fig. 6)

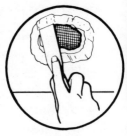

Fig. 6

6. You may need to fill in large holes with wadded newspaper. Start your patching by working in from all sides. Let dry. Apply another layer around new edge. Repeat, until the hole is filled. After the patch has dried, sand until smooth. (Fig. 7)

Fig. 7

NOTE: If the walls have a textured surface, you'll want to make your patch match while the plaster is still wet. You might need a sponge or comb to do the texturing. (Fig. 8)

Fig. 8

STRIPPING WALLPAPER

This can be a wretched task for any landlord; however, with the proper materials, the job can be simplified. Your paint store clerk can recommend a good wallpaper removal solution. You will also need a wide putty knife. Drench all areas and let the solution soak in sufficiently. Then, with a scraping motion, remove the paper with a putty knife.

SETTING TILE

You may need to replace tiles from walls or floors because they are damaged or missing. You will need a mixing bowl, tile adhesive, a knife or saw, new tiles, grout for ceramic or plastic tile, and an iron.

Flexible Tile:

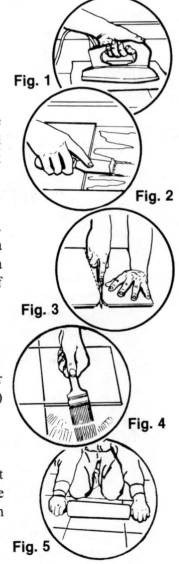

1. Remove any loose or damaged tile. A warm iron will help soften the adhesive. (Fig. 1)

Fig. 1

2. Scrape off the old adhesive from the floor or wall, and from the tile if you plan to use it again. (Fig. 2)

Fig. 2

3. Fit tiles carefully into place. Some tiles can be cut with a knife or shears, others with a saw. Tile is less apt to break if warm. (Fig. 3)

Fig. 3

4. Spread adhesive on the floor or wall with a putty knife. (Fig. 4)

Fig. 4

5. Wait until adhesive begins to set before placing the tile. Put tile firmly in place. (A rolling pin works well.) (Fig. 5)

Fig. 5

Ceramic or Plastic Tile:

1. Scrape off the old adhesive from floor or wall, and the old tile if you plan to use it again. (Fig. 6)

Fig. 6

2. If you are using new tile which needs fitting, mark it carefully to size. You can make straight cuts on tile by scoring it first. It will then snap off if you press it on the end of a hard surface. (Fig. 7)

3. Spread adhesive on the surface to be tiled, and on the back of the tile. Then press tile firmly into place. (Fig. 8)

Fig. 7

4. Joints on ceramic tile should be filled with grout after tile has set firmly. Mix grout with water to form a stiff paste. Press the mixture into the joints with your fingers. Smooth the surface. (Fig. 9)

5. Carefully remove the excess grout from the tile surface before it dries. (Fig. 10)

Fig. 8

6. Empty excess grout mixture. Clean up surface and tools. (Fig. 11)

7. Let grout dry overnight before it gets wet again.

Fig. 8

Fig. 9   **Fig. 10**   **Fig. 11**

REPAIRING SCREENS

Repairing existing screens is more economical than buying new ones. This prevents small holes from getting larger and keeps those pesky insects out. You will need pre-cut screen patches or old screening, shears, a ruler, a small block of wood for a straight edge, and fine wire or nylon thread.

1. Trim the hole in the screen to make smooth edges. (Fig. 1)

Fig. 1

2. Cut a rectangular patch an inch larger than the hole to be repaired.

3. Remove the outside wires on all four sides of the patch. (Fig. 2)

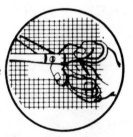

Fig. 2

4. Bend the ends of the wires; they are easily bent over a rock or edge of a ruler. (Fig. 3)

Fig. 3

5. Put a patch over the hole from the outside. Hold it tight against the screen so that the small, bent wire ends go through the screen. (Fig. 4)

6. From inside, bend down the ends of the wires toward the center of the hole and weave them in. You may need someone outside to press against the patch while you do this. (Fig. 5)

NOTE: A small hole may be mended by stitching back and forth with a fine wire or nylon thread. The mending material should match the area. (Fig. 6)

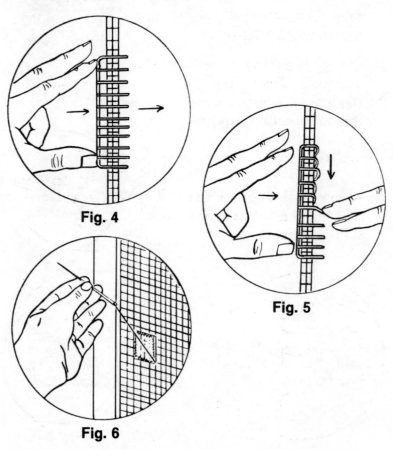

Fig. 4

Fig. 5

Fig. 6

REPAIRING A LEAKY FAUCET

Leaking faucets waste water and cause spots in the sink; also, they can be extremely exhausting because of the constant drip . . . drip . . . drip. What you need is a box of assorted washers (unless you know the exact size), a screwdriver, and an adjustable wrench.

1. Begin first by turning off the water at the shut-off valve nearest to the faucet you are going to repair. (Fig. 1) Then turn on the faucet until the water stops flowing.

2. Loosen the packing nut with adjustable wrench. (Fig. 2) Most nuts loosen by turning counterclockwise. Use the handle to pull out the valve unit. (Fig. 3)

3. Remove the screw holding the old washer at the bottom of the valve unit. (Fig. 4)

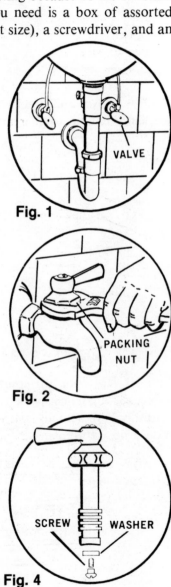

Fig. 1

Fig. 2

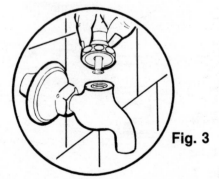

Fig. 3

Fig. 4

4. Put in new washer and replace screw. (Fig. 5)

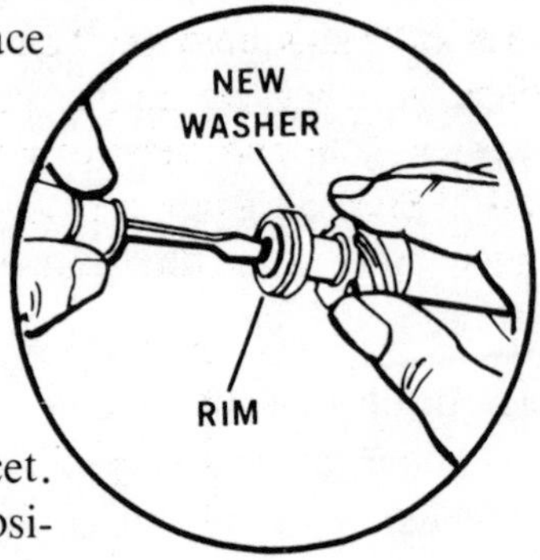

NEW WASHER

RIM

Fig. 5

5. Put valve unit back in faucet. Turn handle to the proper position.

6. Tighten the packing nut. (Fig. 6)

7. Turn on the water at the shut-off valve.

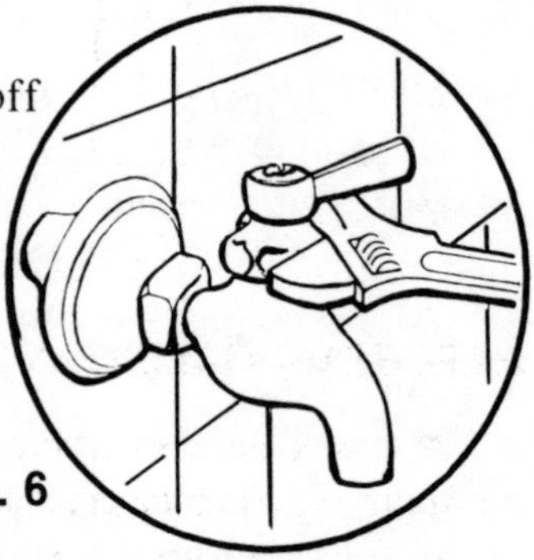

Fig. 6

Faucets may look different, but they are all built about the same. Mixing faucets which are used on sinks, laundry tubs, and bathtubs, are actually two separate units with the same spout. You'll need to repair each unit separately. (Fig. 7)

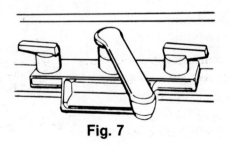

Fig. 7

Is water leaking around the packing nut? Try tightening the nut. If it still leaks, remove the handle and loosen the packing nut. If there is a washer under it, replace the washer. If there's no washer, you may need to wrap the spindle with "packing wicking." (Fig. 8) Then replace packing nut and handle, and turn water back on at the shut-off valve.

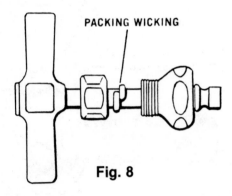

PACKING WICKING

Fig. 8

PATCHING CRACKS AT BATHTUB AND SHOWER

A crack between the bathtub and wall must be repaired to avoid any further damage to the walls or house frame. You will need waterproof grout or plastic sealer. Grout comes in powder form and must be mixed with water. It usually costs less than plastic sealers. Plastic sealer comes in a tube and resembles toothpaste. Although it may cost a little more than grout, it is easier to use. Read directions on the package before starting your project.

1. Begin by removing the old crack filler from the crack. (Fig. 1)

Fig. 1

2. Wash the surface to remove soap, grease and dirt. (Fig. 2)

3. Dry the surface well before you make the repairs. (Fig. 3)

4. When using grout, put a small amount of grout in a bowl. (Fig. 4)

Fig. 2

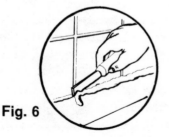

Fig. 3

Fig. 4

5. Slowly add water and continue mixing until you have a thick paste. Put this mixture in the crack with a putty knife. (Fig. 5)

6. Press in to fill the crack. (Fig. 6)

7. Smooth the surface. (Fig. 7)

Fig. 5

Fig. 6

Fig. 7

Wipe excess grout from the wall and tub before it can dry and harden. Then let the grout dry well in the repaired area before allowing anyone to use the tub.

Empty any leftover grout from the mixing bowl (not down the drain). Wash out your bowl and knife before the grout dries on them.

When using plastic sealer, just squeeze the sealer from the tube along the crack. Use a putty knife or spatula to press it down and fill the crack. Smooth the surface. Work very fast — plastic sealer dries in a very few minutes. Keep the cap on the tube when you're not using it. (Fig. 8)

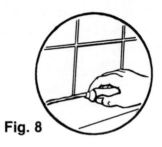

Fig. 8

PAINTING THE INTERIOR

Careless painting wastes time and can be a terrible experience. Proper preparation is necessary to do a good job that will last the years. Buying all your paint and supplies is your first step. Next, wash the walls and woodwork. Fill all cracks and holes, and remove all fixtures and electrical plates. Then cover everything with dropcloths so the room won't be freshly spreckled.

When you paint all your apartments with a standard color, you'll find that it is more economical — it's easier to do touch up work. A standard off-white, like antique white, will eliminate an accumulation of partly-filled paint cans which you can't use because all the colors are different. Off-white makes a room appear larger, fits nicely with almost any furniture scheme, and looks clean.

Over the years, landlords and tenants alike have preferred a satin latex for painting living rooms, hallways, and bedrooms. Semi-gloss enamel is good for kitchens, baths, and woodwork. These paints are scrubable, spread well, are durable, and seldom need repainting.

Before application, prepare the surface by washing with a TSP (trisodium phosphate) solution, then rinse it with clear water. Be sure the furniture as well as the floors are covered with a dropcloth and all electrical plates and switch covers are removed.

A large five-gallon can with a roller panel in it is better than a roller pan. Always do the large wall and ceiling areas first; then finish up with trim and semi-gloss work.

Showing & Renting Apartments

This chapter is delegated to a step-by-step procedure of taking a vacant apartment through all steps necessary to fill it with a qualified, paying tenant. While it may be the greatest available rental in the city, a vacant apartment will remain vacant indefinitely if the public doesn't know it is available. On the other hand, if you fill the unit with an undesirable, non-paying deadbeat, you'll wish the unit was vacant.

The fastest way to bankruptcy, or at least a migraine headache, is to continually rent to non-paying tenants. There are enough qualified prospects to fill your vacant units without attempting financial suicide.

ADVERTISING

Bringing prospects to your door is best accomplished by using vacancy signs and classified advertising. Vacancy signs must be precise and to the point, qualifying the prospective tenant to a certain degree. For example, "Vacancy, 1-bedroom Adults Only," or "Vacancy, 2-bedroom Kids OK." By stating certain important facts about the unit, you will eliminate a lot of unqualified prospects who are looking for something which you don't have available.

Vacancy signs should be legible and large enough so that they can be seen easily from any passing car. Signs must also be placed where they get maximum exposure — either on the side of your building, or posted on the lawn near your busiest street.

Classified advertising should also be precise and qualifying in order to eliminate unnecessary calls from unqualified prospects. The four basic principles of good advertising are "A-I-D-A." 1. ATTENTION . . . Your headline should attract specific prospects. 2. INTEREST . . . Expansion of the headline offering a benefit to the prospect which makes him read the rest of the ad. 3. DESIRE . . . With good descriptive copy, make the prospect want what you have to offer. 4. ACTION . . . Ask for action by making it easy for the prospect to respond to your offer.

ATTENTION . . . could be a heading like "Newly decorated" or "Large 2-Bedroom." The purpose of the attention heading is to get the reader to distinguish your ad from all the other ads in the column.

INTEREST . . . must offer a benefit like "New dishwasher," Newly carpeted" or "Great Ocean View". This will entice the reader to finish reading the remainder of your offer.

DESIRE . . . will describe precisely what you have to offer. Like "2-Bedroom, Kids-OK, $225, or 1-Bedroom, Adults Only, Pool, $195."

ACTION . . . can be simply a phone number for the reader to call and inquire.

Classified ads are "classified" under specific headings and there is no need to duplicate information that is already available. In other words, it isn't necessary to state that your apartment is unfurnished when you are advertising in the unfurnished apartment column, or stating that you are downtown in a column denoting specific areas.

2-BEDROOM APARTMENT in downtown
area. New wall-to-wall carpeting and drapes.

YOUR TENANT PROFILE

Families with children like to live in a building where other families have children. Likewise, adults without children prefer to live where only adults reside. Senior citizens enjoy living with other older folks and singles prefer living with other (young) singles. Therefore, you must determine what your tenant profile will be in your buildings. The reason for utilizing a tenant profile is to eliminate the costly turnover of tenants. You can reduce turnover by keeping the same character of clientele as tenants in each of your buildings. Your tenants will develop lasting neighbors within each complex, which in turn will keep them happier and eliminate tenants moving away from varying tenant life styles.

In other words, only rent to one specific category of people. If you decide on a family building and continue to allow singles to move in, you'll find that most of your time is spent putting up vacancy signs.

Now that you have located your vacancy sign properly and your classified advertising is running in the daily newspaper, it is time to market your units to the prospects. In order to successfully sell your vacant unit to qualified potential tenants, your resident manager's responsibilities are to know the following information in order to answer questions about the units available. He should also be knowledgeable about area, schools, churches, etc.

1. Size of apartment, square footage, various layouts available.
2. Sizes of individual rooms.
3. Closet space, linen space, cupboard space.
4. Equipment: refrigerator, stove, disposal, type of heating, air conditioner, furnishings.
5. Amenities: pools, etc.

A resident manager must know the character of the community and what services it has to offer. For example:
1. Income level of the residents.
2. Noise level of the area.

3. Shopping center locations.
4. Transportation.
5. Highway routes.
6. Recreation areas.
7. Points of interest.
8. Educational facilities.

When the prospect is being shown about by the manager, it is imperative that the vacant unit is spic and span. Dirt costs money. That empty unit will be much easier to fill when it appears bright and new.

Should your units have disadvantages about them, do not allow the manager to bring those facts up. What may be a disadvantage to some may not be to others. In other words, let the sleeping dragons rest.

COMPETITION

You, as an owner, will face two different types of competition in supplying housing to the public. Direct competition prevails when other buildings in the area offer similar space at equivalent rental rates to your own building. On the other hand, indirect competition is present when different units are present which appeal to a different kind of prospect. For example, a singles-only building with a large pool and tennis courts that exists across the street from your family building without a pool and tennis courts is indirect competition. You are obviously going to attract a different type of clientele.

In direct competition, management will make the difference as to who will make the best profit. Management should create a good working relationship with the indirect competition. Both can gain good, qualified tenants by referring prospects to each other. The resident manager should also visit direct competition every six months because of changing rent schedules and new complexes being built.

RENTING THE APARTMENT

First be sure all who occupy your apartments will fit your tenant profile.

If a complete stranger approached you on the street and said "I need your car — may I have your keys?" you would probably tell him, "No."

In the apartment rental business, there are many managers who will allow a person or family to move into an apartment who comes in off the street — a complete stranger — and says, in effect, "I need the use of this $20,000 investment — an apartment." This person could be the same stranger who asked for your car, and he hasn't given the manager any information about himself.

Yet, time after time, a tenant will acquire possession of an asset worth thousands of dollars with no more identification or background check than showing up at the manager's door and saying, "I need a place to live."

He then gains possession plus much, much more — whether or not he decides to pay rent in the future, he has gained the right to use and enjoy your property and the right of privacy.

Should your new tenant not pay rent and the owner wishes him removed from the premises, it must be done by "due process of law." In California, it is an Unlawful Detainer action. In most other states, it is an Eviction suit. These actions, if successful, will only bring a judgement for rent monies, court costs, and moving fees. Cases that go to court will undoubtedly require 20-30 days or more. The costs involved, plus additional loss of rent, can get out of hand when a professional deadbeat decides to slither onto your premises.

The only way to avoid the professional deadbeat is to properly check prospective tenant backgrounds. It is best to join a local association, which is equipped to render a credit checking service.

Once a prospect is checked and found to be unworthy of your standards, do not tell the prospect the source of your information, only that "the information we obtained does not meet our requirements."

After the manager has shown the prospect about the building and the individual looks like a likely candidate to be a good tenant, the manager must ask for the rental if the prospect hasn't asked to rent it, as it can't be assumed. He might ask, "When would be a good time for you to move in?" If the prospect decides he wants the unit, have him leave a minimum of a $50 deposit to hold the vacant unit. This deposit acts to commit the prospect to a promise. It also is good to have in case the prospect later changes his mind. In that case, you at least have an opportunity to resell him when he returns to pick up the deposit.

LEASE AGREEMENTS

Tenancy — the relationship between owner and tenant is created, operated, and terminated under very specific laws in each state. You will be primarily involved with fixed and periodic tenancy. *Fixed Tenancy* is, in effect, for a specific period of time, such as one year. Fixed tenancy has an exact starting date and a specific duration. It is not renewed or extended without agreement by both parties. Rent payments do not necessarily coincide with the term of tenancy. Thus, if a tenancy is for one year, rent is usually paid on a monthly or yearly basis during that year.

Periodic tenancy involves a continuous series of terms, rather than a single term. Each term is automatically renewed, unless one of the parties gives notice to terminate the tenancy. An example is a typical month-to-month tenancy, where occupation runs for one month, then starts over and runs for another month. Rent is paid usually on a month-to-month basis. If a tenant doesn't vacate after a month, tenancy becomes periodic when the owner acknowledges the fact by accepting rent.

A lease, in addition to being a contract, is a conveyance or transfer of property rights and it must contain the following: form, intention, delivery and terms.

The form of a lease can either be verbal or written. Every state sets differing limitations. A lease must be in writing if it exceeds a specific term. The following applies to the State of California:

1. A lease for a term of one year or more must be in writing.

2. A lease to start in the future for term of one year or more must be in writing.
3. The transfer or assignment of a lease to another tenant for term longer than one year must be in writing.

Some states allow the use of verbal leases. However, I recommend all leases be in writing. It is extremely foolish for an owner to get involved with verbal leases and leave everything to chance for the following reasons: 1) a written lease is easier to prove in court; 2) it prevents misunderstanding and clarifies terms; 3) it can discourage subletting, and 4) it is easier to claim damages.

SIGNATURES ON THE LEASE

A lease should be signed by the tenant, the tenant's spouse, and all adults who will occupy the premises. Where two, three or more are sharing the apartment, a clause of "tenants are jointly and severally responsible for payment of rent," is required.

If the manager signs the lease for the owner, signature should appear as follows:

John Doe
_____
Owner

by Helen Dupa
_____
Manager

A lease must be delivered to take effect.

In order for a lease to be legal, it must show the following:
1. Complete legal names of all parties involved.
2. That it is intended to be a lease and that it establishes an owner/tenant relationship.
3. A complete description of the property.
4. Amount of rent to be paid and when.
5. Term of lease to be in effect.

If the tenant remains in the residence after the lease expires and the owner accepts rent, tenancy is changed to the term for which the rent is paid, becoming a periodic tenancy of month-to-month or week-to-week.

Usage and custom in the United States have established that rents are payable in advance. Rents are normally due at the end of any payment period, unless otherwise stated in the lease.

ASSIGNING OR TRANSFERRING A LEASE

A tenant may assign or transfer his lease to another person unless a provision in the lease prevents it. In order to protect the owner, it is imperative that a provision is written so that tenant cannot sell, transfer, or assign the lease without consent of the owner in writing.

EXISTING TENANTS

At the onset of taking over management of a building, be sure all existing tenants are under a written rental agreement. In the case of leasing furnished units, make appointments with the tenants and make an inventory of all furniture. Have the tenant sign the inventory and new rental agreement at the same time.

DEPOSITS

Apart from rent, before right of possession is given to the tenant, certain deposits will be necessary to insure an apartment's successful operation. A security deposit is a refundable deposit protecting the owner from damage to the premises. A good rule of thumb on a month-to-month tenancy is to charge one month's rent for security. This amount can be adjusted upwards, depending upon additional furnishings the owner may supply. Prior to a move-in, a tenant should be informed that the security deposit cannot be applied to his rent. It will be refunded when the apartment is vacated if proper notice is given and the apartment is left in good condition.

Another deposit is the non-refundable cleaning fee. This charge generally runs between $50 and $100 depending on the character of the building. Certain states do not allow a cleaning fee to be charged. If that is the case, you may simply rename the charge to a one-time leasing charge, non-refundable.

A key deposit is also a necessary charge, refundable when the apartment is vacated and keys returned intact. A good, nominal key deposit fee to charge incoming tenants is $10.

Additional deposits should be charged if you decide to allow pets on the premises. Suggested fee for pet damage deposit is $100 - $200.

RENT COLLECTION

Profitably managing your real estate will invariably depend on your collection policies. A good collection policy begins by properly qualifying a tenant before he moves in. This will avoid many costly headaches as it filters out most of the professional deadbeats. Before giving out keys and handing over possession, it is imperative that all deposits and rent in advance is collected. There is no reason for anything less.

Your apartment building investment is purely a money-making business, not a downtown mission run on charity. Owners who yield to nonpaying deadbeats cannot meet their own operating costs and will soon end up in bankruptcy.

Rents can be collected very efficiently when the resident manager and tenants are aware of the procedures and they are followed. A good collection policy is to have all rent payable due dates effective the first seven days of the month. Exceptions can be made in regard to paydays.

Effective contract forms should be used. A triplicate rent receipt form is necessary with a copy each for tenant (should he ask for it), resident manager, and owner. A reminder notice is to be used when rent is three days past due. If your tenant does not respond to a three-day notice, the manager must then make a personal visit to collect, and, if no progress is made on the personal visit, a Three-Day Pay Rent or Quit the Premises Notice must be issued immediately. (See evictions chapter for more data on a three-day notice.)

Many sophisticated property managers charge a $10 fee when rent is more than three days past due. This method is very effective. However, some state laws do not approve. In most cases, I have found that only once do you need to enforce this method; tenants are rarely late again.

Your resident manager should have a sheet at the beginning of each month listing tenants' due dates, rent amounts, and comments. Then as a tenant pays, his name is crossed off the list. This delinquency list serves as a ready reference for both manager and owner. Occasionally, a tenant will tell the manager that the rent will be paid two days late. This remark will be noted on the delinquency list and followed up by the manager in two days.

If after three days the rent has not been paid without specific reason, the manager must attach a three-day reminder to the tenant's door. This should be noted and stated on the delinquency list under comments. Two days after the three-day reminder, the manager must follow up either personally or by phone. If no money or response is given, a Three-Day Notice to Pay or Quit must be issued. Check your local state laws governing this matter of the Pay or Quit Notice.

When a tenant has established a good payment history, more lenient allowances can be made when circumstances occur such as the loss of a job, illness, or death in the family. Whatever the case, definite commitments must be made and recorded on the delinquency sheet and followed up by the manager.

Rent payments must be made in the form of check or money order — absolutely no cash. This will eliminate any temptation of theft or a manager's possible desires to borrow small amounts of cash. Only in the case of emergency or when someone is extremely late in paying his rent should hard-cash be accepted.

Instead of a late fee to stimulate prompt payment, efficient managers often utilize a $10 discount from rent if paid within two days of due date. If you decide to use this effective method, you can offset the $10 loss merely by charging $10 more when you originally rent the apartment. The base rent would then be equal to the discounted rate.

HOW TO RAISE RENTS

At the initial stage of taking over the responsibility of managing a building, it will probably be necessary to raise rents on most of the units. Rental increases for existing tenants are handled the same as changing any other terms of tenancy. In most states the law requires a minimum of 30-day notice to inform tenants of the new rental rate. I recommend giving a 45-day notice to allow more consideration for your tenants.

When raising rents, you must always be concerned with the fact that some tenants may decide to move, especially if they can find less expensive comparable housing. Therefore, it is very important that you know what comparable housing is renting for. If you keep rent raises equal to or below comparable units in the area, the majority of your tenants being raised will surely remain. The cost of moving and the hassle is too much to bear just to find similar housing for the same price.

To avoid the possibility of having a large amount of vacant units all at one time, you must *not* send out rent raise letters to the entire building all at the same time. Raise no more than 25% of the building the first month and a similar number each month until you have all the units at comparable rates. The best and easiest time to raise rents is when a vacancy occurs.

For an example of a rent raise letter, see chapter on "Forms."

Under specific lease agreements, rents cannot be raised during the term of the lease. You are only eligible to raise the rent at the expiration of the lease.

The Resident Manager

Once a property is purchased and basic improvements and rental increases have been accomplished, an apartment owner only has to spend a few hours a month on any individual property. When a competent resident manager is on the premises, he can relieve the owner of many time-consuming operations and responsibilities. On the other hand, an incompetent manager can create nagging headaches and needless expense.

In order to reach the stage where only a few hours per month are put into each property, you, the owner must delegate as much responsibility to your resident manager as you possibly can. When this is accomplished, it will require you to make only major decisions. Then you can devote your time to policies involving your entire estate and find that apartment ownership is more of a breathtaking challenge than a daily chore.

After the initial acquisition of a property, you must decide whether to keep the existing manager or find a new one. Usually, 30 days is enough time to determine the capabilities of the existing manager. Should you not be satisfied with the current manager, it is best to begin looking for a replacement immediately. Good managers are plentiful if you need a replacement, as you will soon find out.

Certain ingredients make for an ideal resident manager. A husband and wife are ideally suited for apartments if, for example, the husband works full time at a normal job and the wife is free to manage. Following are the chief qualities found in a good manager, listed in their order of importance:

1. Eagerness and willingness to do the job properly.
2. Ability to accept responsibility.
3. A husband that is handy at minor repairs.
4. A wife with a pleasant personality and a willingness to stay at home and assist in the overall maintenance of the property.
5. Honesty.
6. Experience.

Please note that "experience" is listed last in priority. Many times I have found that it takes more time to weed out so-called experienced managers and their inefficiencies than it takes to completely train an inexperienced manager.

Primarily, the manager's responsibility is to collect rents, show vacant apartments, and keep the grounds clean. A husband who may have a full-time job elsewhere can operate as a handyman for minor repairs and lawn mowing. It isn't always necessary to call on a skilled repairman to do minor repairs.

It is very important that the manager is on the job to show vacancies and keep order. A wife that is overly active socially outside the home is not a good prospect, while the domestic housewife with children tends to be the best "stay-at-home."

What you pay the manager depends primarily on the size of the building. With a 20 unit building, free rent would be a typical agreement. On a smaller four-plex type building, 25% to 33% of rent on a one-bedroom apartment (depending on the rental rate) would be normal. Buildings larger than 20 units usually involve free rent plus cash salaries. Look in the classified section of your local newspaper under the column "Couples Wanted" for competitive rates and salaries.

SUPERVISING YOUR MANAGER

Duties of the resident manager must be fully explained at the outset of the owner-employee relationship. Remember, the more responsibility an owner can delegate to the manager, the more time he has to pursue other matters.

Monthly reports are absolutely necessary for proper accounting and ready reference. These reports include a list of rents collected, one copy of each rent receipt, delinquency list, and bank deposit. Larger buildings may include other forms reporting vacancies, future available apartments, etc.

Each entry in a list of rents collected should include apartment number, rent paid date and due date, amount paid, and type of money paid (rent, cleaning fee, key deposit or security deposit). One copy of each rent receipt is attached to rent collected sheet and one given to the owner. A copy of rent receipt is also kept on file by the manager and the tenant receives the third copy (if requested).

The delinquency report is kept by the manager for ready reference. This form will denote apartment numbers, tenant names, amount due, and a column for comments. At the first of the month, the manager will fill out each apartment number, name, and amount due; he then crosses off each tenant as the rent is paid. Comment column is used for noting the date when a late tenant promises to pay, or the date when delinquent notices were issued. The delinquency form is an excellent tool for efficient collection work.

Bank deposit copies or reports are optional, depending on whether the manager or the owner make bank deposits. By the way, I would like to reemphasize, major expenses should be billed directly to the owner. Establishing regular charge accounts with various suppliers will avoid a manager padding bills or receiving kickbacks from sales people.

Monthly supervisory visits by the owner are a good practice. Major decisions of recarpeting or other costly repairs can be accomplished, plus, picking up collected rents and a periodic inspection can be done in one visit. Immediately after a new acquisition, you'll spend more time than usual on the property, but, as time goes by, your time will be better spent elsewhere.

Budgeting

The successful operation of all your buildings will greatly depend on a carefully planned budget, then sticking to it without exception. Financial planning of all income and expenses will avoid a cash shortage situation which will inevitably destroy an otherwise healthy business. What seems to always occur when owners do not plan properly, is deferred maintenance . . . which causes vacancies . . . which in turn causes loss of revenue and further deferred maintenance. Loss in value of the entire asset will eventually occur as deferred maintenance will take its toll over the years as needed upkeep allocations are placed elsewhere. Improper handling of funds can also lead to a tax sale as the property is unable to meet its tax requirements. Or, if an owner is short of cash, he has to accept an offer of purchase for less than he would normally accept under a healthy financial condition.

Budgeting not only encompasses the planning of income and expense, but also the future replacement of expensive capital items. Carpets, drapes, appliances and furniture are among the most common items that need replacing. Often a roof or a water heater seems to need repair when you least expect it. These are items that can't wait to be repaired and the cost usually starts in the neighborhood of $800 or more. Careful planning and budgeting will allow you to pay for these items when needed, not deferring the repair work to a point where good paying tenants begin to move out.

The budget begins when you initially take over the operation of a building. Take the existing operating statement from the past owner or manager from whom you assumed control and make adjustments to all the income and expense categories. There are certain expense items which will remain constant, such as property taxes and mortgage payments. Areas where improvements can be made are usually in vacancy percentages, management, and repairs and maintenance.

Sample Income and Expense items to be budgeted

Projected Income:
Rent
Laundry
Expenses:
Taxes
Debt Service
Gas
Water
Electricity
Insurance
Management
Advertising
Supplies
Vacancy Allowance
Pest Control
Gardener
Maintenance and Repairs

You must set aside a contingency fund for future outlays of cash, besides general expenses, in the areas of capital items. For example, carpeting usually has to be replaced every five years. New, medium quality carpet with installation included costs about $500 per apartment. Therefore, it requires $100 per year, per unit, for a replacement reserve contingency fund for carpeting, or approximately $8 per month. A similar replacement reserve fund must be set aside for drapes and roofing, furniture and appliances. Useful lives of these various capital items differ depending on quality. The Internal Revenue Service has a guide available for useful life of capital items. Usually, capital items have the following ranges of useful life: carpeting and appliances, five to seven years; drapes, three to five years; and a roof 10 - 20 years.

ALLOCATION FOR REPLACEMENT RESERVES

The best procedure to budget these items is to estimate total outlay for all future capital expenditures, keeping the contingency fund for each item in a savings account to use when the money is required. Itemize each particular expense or replacement reserve which will require a large future expenditure as shown in the sample on the next page. Then, a monthly estimate is set aside in a savings account for that day when the expenditure will be required.

To give you a sample of how we arrive at a monthly estimate to set aside, I will break down an example of replacement reserves for carpeting. Lets assume a cost of $500 to replace carpeting in one individual unit of a 10-unit building with a carpet life of five years. If we divide $500 by five years, then divide that result by 12 months, we have a monthly allocation for carpeting one unit of approximately $8 per unit.

The following items are for your use in making future estimates to set aside for monthly replacement reserves.

Taxes: 1/12th of annual tax bill per month. Be sure to project for any possible future increase by your tax assessor.

Insurance: 1/12th of annual insurance permium.

Carpeting: $8 per month per unit. This represents an estimate of $500 for cost of carpeting installed for an average apartment with a useful life of five years.

Furniture: In the absence of actual costs for replacement of furniture, estimate $350 for a single or bachelor unit, $500 for a one-bedroom, and $600 for a two-bedroom. To arrive at a monthly figure, simply divide by five years, then by 12 for a monthly reserve for furniture.

Roof: Estimate about $8 per month per unit.

Drapes: $2 per month per unit.

Interior Painting: $4 per month per unit.

Misc. General Repairs: $2 per month per unit.

Mechanical Equipment: Water heaters, elevators, etc. Determine cost and useful life, then calculate the monthly reserve needed.

Now that you have all the items pertinent to your building estimated on a monthly basis, you can add them and arrive at a total to set aside each month.

Evictions

Regardless of whether you do your own evictions or have someone else do them, you should know a lawyer to consult when there are legal entanglements. In most cases you can save a ton of money doing it yourself, but a good lawyer is indispensable.

Lawyers will take more time with evictions than you would for a number of reasons. First, they will usually try to go to court with more than one case, which will delay your specific case. Second, you will usually delay handing the case over to a lawyer because of the expense involved and trying to believe the tenants excuses, hoping he will move out before you spend eviction money. And third, a lawyer doesn't have the incentive of money that you do to speed the eviction process through.

This chapter will acquaint you with forms, procedures, costs and everything involved with doing an eviction yourself. Doing it yourself will cost about $60. If your time is worth more than your money, hire a lawyer to handle your evictions.

Two basic situations will present themselves where it will be necessary for you to evict a tenant . . . either non-payment of rent or terminating tenancy due to breach of contract. Breach of contract includes unauthorized pets, too much noise, more people living in the apartment than originally agreed upon, etc.

The following are situations based on eviction procedures in the State of California. Other states have similar procedures; it's best to check your local landlord-tenant laws.

EVICTION FOR NON-PAYMENT OF RENT

This type of eviction, like all other evictions, begins with a written notice served to the tenant. It is called a "Three-Day Notice to Pay Rent or Quit the Premises." (See examples of a Three-Day Notice in chapter on forms.) A Three-day Notice is properly served in one of three ways: 1. Deliver it to the tenant personally. 2. Mail a copy by certified mail, plus deliver it to someone else on the premises of a suitable age, or to tenant at the place of his employment. 3. Send a copy by certified mail and post a copy at the door where it is unavoidable.

The first method is best, but after repeated attempts, other methods may be used. If your deadbeat tenant refuses to accept the notice, that's his problem. You need only notify him that he's being served and where he can see the notice.

To be legally binding, a correct Three-day Notice to Pay Rent or Quit the Premises must contain the following items:

1. Correct name of the tenant served.
2. Address of the subject dwelling.
3. Total amount of rent due.
4. Period of time for which rent is due.
5. Your signature as owner or resident manager as agent.

All the above information must be correct and consistent. Be sure to include rent due for the current rental period. For example, if you serve the notice on the first of July because rent was not paid for the month of June, include July's rent, too. You are now in the current July rental period. If you serve the notice on the 28th day of June, it shouldn't include July's rent.

Once a Three-Day Notice to Pay or Quit is served, the tenant has to make a choice — pay up or move out. If he pays in full, your problems are over. If he attempts to pay you a partial payment and you accept it, the Three-day Notice is no longer valid. If he doesn't pay the balance, you must begin the Three-day Notice process all over again. To be successful, it is wise only to accept full payment.

If after three days the tenant has not utilized either alternative to pay up or move out, then you must begin an Unlawful Detainer action against him.

TRY TO AVOID COURT

After being served a notice, most tenants begin to realize the severity of their predicament and are willing to negotiate a settlement without going to court. Settle, by all means, and avoid going to court if you can. You will avoid having your property tied up unprofitably, as time is on the tenant's side. Be reasonable. If the tenant needs time to move, offer to help him store bulky things. However, if you feel it is necessary, proceed with the eviction without delay.

UNLAWFUL DETAINER

This procedure is initiated after the tenant has been served with a Three-Day Notice to Pay or Quit and has not complied with the notice and the proper 3-day period has elapsed. It is now time to file the Summons and Complaint in Municipal Court.

The Summons is a written notice to the tenant that he is being sued and that he must respond to the Complaint within five days. If the tenant does not respond within five days, he risks almost certain eviction. Blank Summons forms are available at your Municipal court clerk's office. You, the landlord, need to fill out only the front side of the Summons, while the Process Server will fill in the back side as proof of service.

Telephone the clerk of the Municipal Court for the city where your property is located and ask for the following information:

1. Is your property within the jurisdiction of that particular court?

2. What is the filing fee?
3. What is the exact location of the court?

With this information you can fill out the front half of the Summons only. Make one copy from the original Summons and one additional copy for each defendant.

The Complaint must be prepared for filing along with the Summons. The Complaint reviews your contract with the tenant, states your case against him, asks the court to return the premises to you, and requests a money judgement to cover amount owed, including costs and any damages.

Your Complaint should be typed on legal paper (8½" x 14") with numbers down the side, following a legal format. For a simple Unlawful Detainer involving nonpayment of rent, use the sample form in the chapter on forms. Fill in the appropriate information that is relevant to your case.

Now that the Summons and Complaint are prepared, type "Exhibit A" atop a copy of the Notice served to the tenant and attach it to your Complaint.

FILING THE SUMMONS AND COMPLAINT

Take the correct number of copies of your Summons and Complaint to the Municipal Court Clerk's office which you telephoned earlier for information. Try to arrive in the morning so the Process Server will have the opportunity to serve the papers the same day.

The clerk will require originals and copies of both forms, and the filing fee. He will then assign a number to your case, open a corresponding file, and return to you a receipt for the filing fee. While you have the opportunity, get some advice from the clerk regarding serving your tenant. Practices vary throughout the country and any recommendations may be helpful.

WHO MAY SERVE AND WHEN TO SERVE

Any of the following may serve the Summons and Complaint:
1. A Sheriff or Marshal.

2. A professional Process Server.
3. Someone you know, not you, who is at least 18 years old.

You, acting as the plaintiff, are legally forbidden to serve the Summons and Complaint. I recommend a uniformed Sheriff or Marshal to serve the papers. It appears more legally overpowering and intimidating to the tenant. It also helps to avoid the tenant answering the Complaint. If he does answer, it will cost you more time.

A Sheriff or Marshal's office usually can be found in the same building as the court, or reasonably close by. A professional Process Server can be found in the Yellow Pages. In some cases they can work on weekends and save you some time.

The best time to serve a Three-Day Notice is anytime Sunday or Monday.

The best time to serve a Three-Day Notice to perform a covenant, (a notice for breach of contract by the tenant whereas the tenant is doing something he agreed not to do or vice versa,) is shortly after the rent has been paid. Since the tenant expects to be evicted, he will not be eager to pay any rent after the notice has been served. If the case goes to court, you should lose no rent at all if you served the notice properly, shortly after the rent was paid.

The best time to serve a Thirty-Day Notice is also shortly after the rent has been paid. Again, once a tenant knows he's not wanted, his will to pay strongly diminishes. It is possible to lose some rent if your tenant decides to stay over after the 30 days and on into the eviction proceedings, but it will be less than you could lose if you delay longer in serving.

SUBSTITUTED SERVICE

When it comes time for your tenant to be served and he cannot be located, the Process Server must revert automatically to the second or third methods which are the same for serving a Thirty-Day Notice as for a Three-Day Notice. Hand it to someone else on the property of a suitable age and mail a copy by certified mail, or post the notice by the main entrance of the property and mail a copy by certified mail. Both these alternatives delay things a bit because you need an additional copy for each defendant served under substituted service and your tenant has 15 days to answer the complaint instead of five days.

WHAT IF AN ANSWER HAS BEEN FILED

It is extremely unlikely that an answer to the Complaint will be filed in an Unlawful Detainer for nonpayment of rent, or for termination of tenancy. Because it requires the tenant either to prepare a written answer himself or hire an attorney to do it. That means he must file an Answer with the court and pay a filing fee. Most tenants are unwilling to spend the time and money necessary to file an Answer when they know they will lose the case anyway.

If by chance an Answer has been filed, you'll need to request a trial date using a form which is available through your Municipal Court Clerk. Instead of cluttering up more pages with sample forms, I intend only to recommend asking advice from your Municipal Court Clerk. Practice and procedures vary somewhat from state to state and besides, 93% of all Unlawful Detainer actions receive no Answer. Let's hope you are lucky enough to have no Answer filed.

COURT PROCEDURES

When it's time for your case to be heard, the judge will call you forward to be sworn in. He may then ask you a few questions regarding your rental agreement or amount of judgment you requested. The judge will consider all the facts, then grant the amount of judgment. You may request which day the eviction will occur, which is usually within seven days after the day you appeared in court.

Thank the court for the judgment and then go to the Court Clerk for your completed, judgment form. Now you have to fill in the amount of judgment on the Writ of Execution form. Take the Writ of Execution and the judgment form to the Clerk's office and pay the fee to file a Writ.

Now you have completed all the court related work to regain possession of your beloved property. The next step is to see the Sherrif or Marshal and give him the Writ of Execution, which is the authority to evict the tenant(s) and return the property to you. You must also pay a fee for this service.

The Marshal will then set a date and time of eviction, which should be within seven days, and tell you to appear at that time and to be prepared to take over possession.

Usually you will find that most tenants will disappear just prior to bodily eviction. Keep track of your tenants in case they do move, so you can notify the Marshal and save a needless trip.

If your tenant(s) and their possessions are still on the premises when the Marshal arrives, the tenants will be bodily removed if they don't leave of their own free will. The Marshal will then post a notice declaring the unit has been returned to your possession and that the evictee may not enter the premises without penalty of arrest.

You must now change locks and arrange for tenants to move out their possessions. In California, the practice is to store the furnishings until demanded for return by the tenant, charging only for storage. You must keep the goods for at least 15 days before putting them up for sale, and you must advertise the sale in a local newspaper at least five days prior to the sale. Proceeds from the sale are applied first to the cost of holding the sale, then to the judgment. Whatever is left must be returned to the tenants.

It is very unlikely that eviction proceedings will ever go this far, but you should have a good idea of what to do in case they do.

COLLECTING THE JUDGEMENT

Now that you have legally evicted your flakey deadbeat, you're still out of pocket all that rent money, plus court costs. In many cases, it will be next to impossible to collect a cent. However, you can give the bum a crummy credit rating so if he ever tires to correct his credit, you will be paid. Also, it puts him on the record as having unworthy credit which enables others not to trust him. Authorizing a collection agency to collect for you will automatically give this tenant a poor credit record.

Collection agencies charge 50% of all they collect, and if they don't collect anything, they get nothing for themselves. You can assist a collection agency by offering them all pertinent data necessary regarding the tenant's past history from the rental application.

It is possible to handle the collection yourself by garnishing wages or attaching assets, but I wouldn't recommend it. Let a collection agency handle all the dirty work. You have much better things to do.

Keeping Records

It is very important that you start off on the right foot with a good record keeping system. It is not enough to simply create written records of everything; your records must be organized so the information is easily accessible when needed, especially when tax time arrives.

Begin by having a totally separate set of records for each building you own or operate. Make up file folders and label them for each building: "General Records," "Tenant Records," "Receipts and Expenses." In the General Records file folder, keep anything pertaining to the building as a whole, such as insurance policies, taxes, notes and deeds. In the Tenant Record folder, keep all rental applications, rental agreements, and any particular data pertaining to the tenants. These papers should be kept for at least one year after tenants move out for credit rating or landlord inquiries. In the receipt folder, keep all paid receipts for all expenses related to the building. When tax time comes, you can arrange them chronologically. They must then be stored for a minimum of five years, in case you are audited by the IRS.

TENANT RECORD (CARDEX)

A tenant record, or cardex, is an approximately 5½″ × 8″ index card, used in duplicate — one for the manager on the premises, the other for the owner. It is a ready reference of all monies paid and due and is best kept in a drawer-type cardex holder. (See sample of cardex in forms section). Whenever a tenant makes a payment, it is recorded on the cardex of the manager. Owner then transfers all data onto his cardex from the manager's monthly report of income.

Sample of "Cardex"

PROJ. NAME _____ # _____ PARK # _____

Orig. Move-In Date _____

Lease   Dated _____ Exp. _____

Tenant Tel. No. _____

			Security Deposit	Cleaning Fee	Key Deposit #	Base Rent		Total Rent	Balance Due
DEPOSIT									
RENT POTENTIAL									

Date Due	Date Paid	Receipt Number	Paid To Noon	Amount Paid						

BLDG. # _____ APT. _____ NAME _____ Date Due _____

RECEIPT BOOK

Triplicate receipts will be needed for efficient operation, to be kept on the premises by your resident manager. Whenever money is accepted by the manager, a receipt must be given to the tenant (top copy/original). The second copy goes to the owner along with the monthly income statement, and the third copy stays in the book for the manager's reference. This form notes a tenant's name, date paid, type of money accepted (cash, check or money order), and money defined (rent, security deposit, cleaning, or key deposit). The receipt number is recorded on the cardex along with all other information required on the cardex.

JOURNAL OF INCOME AND EXPENSES

This is basically a record-keeping book in which you will post all income and expense data monthly. A separate journal is necessary for each building. It will allow you ready access to all the information you need to operate income producing property. It includes sections on income, expenses, depreciation, loans, and insurance.

The first section will have a separate sheet for rental and laundry income. The sample form on the next page extends only to the month of June. In a normal journal book, the page extends to December.

Use a felt-tip highlighter to make all your total lines easier to see.

If there is enough room on the page, use the same record sheets for subsequent years by listing the units again further down the page. This way you have the advantage of instant access to past years for comparison purposes. You can then determine when you last raised rents and how much vacancy factor was created by doing so.

The second section is for recording of expenses. Now all those receipts you've been keeping in a file folder are recorded here on a month-to-month basis. Anything you do not have receipts for can be recorded from your checking account record.

54

Monthly Income Record

Page   # _____
Location _____
Year _____

Unit #	Jan	Feb	Mar	Apr	May	Jun
1	225	225	225	225	225	225
2	250	250	250	250	250	250
3	250	250	250	250	250	250
4	200	200	200	200	200	200
5	225	225	225	225	225	225
6	200	200	200	200	200	200
Totals	1350	1350	1350	1350	1350	1350

Laundry _____

Keep in mind that the mortgage payment is not entirely an expense. That portion which goes toward equity is actually an investment, not an expense. Only that portion known as "interest" is an expense.

As soon as you have completed one page, start another expense and payment record by bringing a balance forward to your new sheet. Then start posting your latest entries. After you have entered your last expenditure of the year, total the last sheet and you'll have your annual expenses for each category of your building.

Be careful not to post items on your expense record like new carpeting or the repair of a roof. These are depreciable items, not expenses. Depreciable items are capital improvements that have an extended useful life. A depreciable item, like new carpeting, has a useful life of about five years. In writing off the cost of that improvement, you would write off the cost over a five-year useful life using varying forms of depreciation.

Expense and Payment Record

	Date	Paid to	For	1 Total Paid	2 Mort Prin.	3 Int	
1.	2/1	BANK	1ST MORT.	760.00	122.80	427.20	
2.	2/1	J. LOOT	2ND	125.00	92.40	32.60	
3.	2/3	35 HDWARE	PARTS	9.60			
4.	2/7	LA WATER	WATER	56.71			
5.	2/8	MUN. CT.	EVICTION	21.50			
6.	3/1	BANK	1ST MORT	760.00	124.06	425.94	
7.	3/1	J. LOOT	2ND	125.00	93.01	31.99	
8.							
9.							

	4 Taxes	5 Ins.	6 Mgmt.	7 Repair Maint.	8 Misc.	
1.	120.00	90.00				
2.						
3.				9.60		
4.					UTIL 56.71	
5.					21.50	
6.	120.00	90.00				
7.						
8.						
9.						

DEPRECIATION RECORD

Depreciable items are usually large items which are considered improvements that have an extended useful life. Some examples are: carpeting, major equipment, new linoleum, roof replacement, swimming pool, and laundry machines.

Each of the above items must be depreciated on a separate depreciation record sheet, plus a separate sheet for the building itself. Before you start, it may be wise to consult an accountant or a book on doing your taxes. There are varying methods of using depreciation and I plan to be brief on this subject as tax laws change frequently.

Depreciation Record

Location and description of capital improvement:
  3750 Raymond, 19-unit apt. building.

Date acquired:	Jan. 1967
New or used:	Used
Cost or Value:	$200,000
Land value:	$20,000
Salvage value:	0
Depreciable basis:	$180,000
Method of Depreciation:	125% Declining balance
Useful life:	20 years

	Year	Prior Deprec.	Deprec. Balance	% Year Held	Deprec. This yr.
1	1967	0	180,000	100	11,250
2	1968	11,250	168,750	100	10,547
3	1968	10,547	158,203	100	9,888
4	1970	9,888	148,315	100	9,270
5	___				
6	___				
7	___				

The various methods of depreciation are called Straight Line, Declining Balance (125% and 150% of Straight Line), and Sum of the Year's Digits. Once you begin using one particular method you must continue using that method throughout the duration or ownership of that particular building.

Depreciation, by definition, is the reduction in property value from any cause, as long as the property is not used for personal purposes. Land itself is not depreciable, only the improvements on that land. Depreciation reduces the value of an asset by allowing a deduction from income for income tax purposes. It is not an out-of-pocket expense, like property taxes or interest payments; it is strictly a legal form of sheltering income.

First, you must determine the value of the asset you plan to depreciate. Let's say you bought a building for $200,000. The land is worth $20,000, therefore you have $180,000 in building value which can be depreciated over the economic life of the building. Guidelines to determine economic lives of various assets are available in the Internal Revenue Code. Income property can vary from about 10 to 50 years, depending on the building. In our example, we can assume an economic life of 20 years. The value of depreciable property equals $180,000 divided by 20 years, which equals $9,000 per year depreciation.

Straight Line depreciation allows an equal amount of depreciation every year. Using our value of $180,000, $9,000 is deducted every year by dividing $180,000 by 20 years.

The *125% declining balance* method can only be employed for "used" residential income property. This method allows 1.25 times the straight line rate; but the increased rate is applied to decreasing amounts each year, not to the original cost. This results in a higher rate of depreciation in the early years of ownership, and a lower rate in the later years. Take the above example of $9,000 at Straight Line rate times 1.25. This equals $11,250 which is the amount of depreciation allowed the first year. Depreciation allowed the second year would not be based on the cost of $180,000, but on the cost less the amount of depreciation already taken. ($180,000 minus $11,250, which equals $168,750). Then 1/20th, or 5% of $168,750, which is $8,437.50 times 1.25, which equals $10,547 depreciation for the second year.

The *150% declining balance method* is almost the same as 125% method, except that one and a half times the straight line method is allowed instead of 1.25. Furthermore, the 150% method is applicable only for the investor who is the "first user." This means the investor must have been responsible for construction of the building or he must have acquired title prior to the units being rented or occupied by tenants.

When an investor uses the accelerated methods, such as 125% and 150% declining balance methods, the first few years of ownership income can, in most cases, be completely sheltered from income taxes. After five years, the accelerated methods will fall below the rate of straight line depreciation. It is at this point in the life of most income producing property that an alert owner considers a sale or trade. Then he re-invests in new acquisitions to begin using the accelerated depreciation methods to their best advantage, that is, their highest levels during the early years of ownership.

ANNUAL STATEMENT OF INCOME

The annual statement of income brings together all incomes and expenses for the whole year. Notice how depreciation, not an out-of-pocket expense, is deducted last for tax purposes. This is the work sheet where you can post all miscellaneous expenses, use of telephone, advertising expenses, etc., and you have a finalized profit or loss figure to give to the Internal Revenue Service.

Annual Statement of Income

Location: 3750 Raymond   Year: 1976

INCOME		
Rent	28,471	
Other	629	
TOTAL INCOME	29,100	29,100
EXPENSES		
Interest	8,410	
Taxes, licenses	4,800	
Utilities	1,812	
Services, repairs	321	
Pest control	120	
Insurance	850	
Management	1,800	
TOTAL EXPENSES	18,113	18,113
NET INCOME (before depreciation)		10,987
Less depreciation		− 11,250
NET INCOME (or LOSS) for tax purposes		(263)

Security and Insurance

The security of your building not only includes the protection of your tenants from vandals and thieves, but also from the threat of fire and other unforeseen disasters.

Each and every individual unit must be secured with a double locking mechanism. A locking type door knob with a key insert, plus a deadbolt device, also opened by a key, will usually be sufficient.

In larger buildings where open court areas are prevalent, gates and fences are advisable to prevent traffic flow from trespassers. Burglars usually will not steal from units where easy exits are not available.

Fire extinguishers are necessary to aid in putting out fires. Place them at strategic locations throughout your building. Be sure to use at least five-pound models of a type appropriate for standard fires. An effective fire extinguisher is one that fights all types of fires, is easy to carry and use, modestly priced and durable, and should not leave a big mess to be cleaned up. Only the dry chemical models fit these specifications in the five-pound model. Anything smaller in size is too easy to steal and anything larger is too difficult to use. The old-fashioned soda-acid models are only effective against paper and wood fires. They actually aggravate a grease fire.

Security also means protecting your investment with the proper insurance against all forms of calamity. The holder of the mortgage on your building will require fire insurance so the loan will be protected in case of fire. Besides fire insurance, you should also have rent protection insurance. This type of insurance will guarantee continued income in case a fire destroys a few of your units and tenants have to move out while the units are repaired. If you do not have rent protection insurance, you will lose all the potential income the units would normally bring while occupied.

If you live in or anywhere near a flood area, be sure to have insurance against water damage. Both rent protection and flood insurance only cost a few extra dollars and can protect you against a total loss.

Seldom will personal injury accidents occur on your property, especially any for which you are held liable: but if you're not insured against personal liability, you could be in for a lot of trouble. In defending yourself in such matters, court costs alone could eat you alive. Add personal liability coverage to your total package of insurance and sleep better at night.

In case you're at a point of management responsibility where you operate more than one building, blanket coverage of your entire estate becomes more economical than separate coverage for each building. Insurance companies offer better rates when you consolidate properties under a single policy.

Forms

The forms in this section are for use as you see fit. You may cut them out and duplicate each page on any type of copy processing equipment.

RENTAL APPLICATION

Last name _____ First _____ Initial _____

Spouse's full name _____

Apt. to be occupied by _____ persons

Present
Address _____

City _____ State _____ Zip _____

How long? _____ months _____ years

Applicant's birthdate _____	Driver's License # _____	Social Security # _____
Spouse's birthdate _____	Driver's License # _____	Social Security # _____

Present
landlord _____ Phone _____

Monthly
payment _____ How long? _____

Previous
landlord _____ Phone _____

Employer's
name _____ How long? _____

Address _____

Position _____ Salary _____

Additional income _____ Source _____

Applicant's closest relative _____

Address _____ Phone _____

Bank _____	Checking Acct. # _____
Credit reference _____	Acct. # _____
Credit reference _____	Acct. # _____
Vehicle _____	License # _____
Vehicle _____	License # _____

Name and address of
referring party _____

_____

Signature of
applicant _____

Date _____

MANAGER'S MONTHLY INCOME REPORT

Name	Apt#	Rent	Sec	Key	Lease	Rec#	Total
Laundry							
Total							

Month & Year _____   Total monies collected

_____

Vacant Apts. _____   _____
New Move-ins _____   Manager

DELINQUENCY REPORT

Tenant Name	Apt. #	Amount	Comments

THREE-DAY REMINDER TO PAY RENT

May we call your attention to the fact that our records show your rent unpaid for the current period.

We would appreciate your prompt payment.

_____
Manager

FIVE-DAY REMINDER TO PAY RENT

We have not received your rent for the period of _____ amounting to $_____ although you were notified in a previous notice.

As we are required to report at once to the owner we are asking for immediate payment.

_____
Manager

NOTICE TO PAY RENT OR QUIT THE PREMISES

TO _____

_____

Within three days after service upon you of this notice, you are hereby required to pay the rent of the premises hereinafter described, of which you now hold possession, amounting to the sum of _____ Dollars, ($_____) at the rental rate of _____ Dollars, ($_____) per month, being the rent due and owing for the month commencing the _____ day of _____, 19____, and _____

_____

or you are hereby required to deliver up possession of the hereinafter described premises, within three days after service on you of this notice to _____, the duly authorized agent of the owner of said premises, or the said owner will institute legal proceedings against you to recover the possession of said premises with all rents due and owing and any damages caused to said premises. The undersigned, as Landlord, hereby declares a forfeiture of the agreement under which you occupy the hereinbelow described premises.

The premises herein referred to are situated in the City of _____, County of_____, State of California and are designated by apartment number, number and street as:

_____

_____

_____

_____

Dated this _____ day of _____, 19____.

By: _____ Name and title

30-DAY NOTICE TO TERMINATE TENANCY

TO _____, **TENANT IN POSSESSION: PLEASE TAKE NOTICE** that you are hereby required within 30 days to remove from and deliver up possession of the premises now held and occupied by you, being those premises situated in the City of _____, County of _____, State of California, commonly known as _____ .

This notice is intended for the purpose of terminating the Rental Agreement by which you now hold possession of the above-described premises, and should you fail to comply, legal proceedings will be instituted against you to recover possession, to declare said Rental Agreement forfeited, and to recover treble rents and damages for the period of the unlawful detention.

Please be advised that your rent on said premises is due and payable up to and including the date of termination of your tenancy under this notice, that being the _____ day of _____ , 1979 _____ . Dated this _____ Day of _____ , 19_____ .

_____
Owner/Manager

EXAMPLE:

COMPLAINT — Unlawful Detainer for non-payment of rent

Your name
Address
City, State, Zip
Phone Number
Plaintiff in Propria Persona

IN THE MUNICIPAL COURT OF _____
JUDICIAL DISTRICT, COUNTY OF _____
STATE OF CALIFORNIA

(Your Name) _____ Plaintiff,

        vs.
(Tenant's Name) _____ Defendant.

NO. _____ Complaint of Unlawful Detainer
_____(Nonpayment of Rent)_____

    Plaintiff complains of defendant and for cause of action alleges:

I.

    That the defendant at all times herein mentioned did and does now reside in the above-described Judicial District.

II.

    That the plaintiff is the owner and entitled to possession of the premises located at _____,
in the City of _____ ,
County of _____ , State of _____ .

III.

    That on the _____ day of _____ 19_____, plaintiff leased to the defendant the said premises; that said lease was from month to month; that defendant agreed to pay to the plaintiff the sum of _____
_____ Dollars per month rental for said premises, payable in advance on the _____ day of each and every month thereafter, current per month rental being the sum of
_____ Dollars.

IV.

That by virtue of said lease said defendant went into possession of said premises and still continues to occupy the same.

V.

That on the _____ day of _____ , 19 _____, the plaintiff caused the defendant to be served with a written notice stating the amount of rent due and requiring payment thereof or possession of the premises within three days after service of the notice. A true copy of said notice is attached hereto, marked Exhibit "A" and made a part hereof.

VI.

That three days have elapsed since the service of said notice on defendant but that no part of said rent, the sum of _____ ____ Dollars, has been paid and that the entire sum is now due, owing and unpaid.

VII.

That the rental value of said premises is $_____ per day, and plaintiff has sustained, and is sustaining, damage in that sum per day by reason of defendant's unlawful detainer.

VIII.

That the defendant refused and does now refuse to surrender possession of said premises and continues in possession thereof without consent or permission of the plaintiff.

WHEREFORE, plaintiff requests judgment for:
1. Restitution of said premises;
2. The sum of _____ dollars rent;
3. Damages at the rate of $_____ per day for as long as defendant continues in possession of said premises without plaintiff's permission;
4. Treble the above amounts;
5. Plaintiff's cost of suit herein;

Such and further relief as to this Court may seem meet and proper.

DATED: _____

(Name of Landlord)

_____

Plaintiff in Pro Per

VERIFICATION

I am the plaintiff in the above-entitled action; I have read the foregoing Complaint of Unlawful Detainer and know the contents thereof; and I certify that the same is true of my own knowledge, except as to those matters which are therein stated upon my information or belief; as to those matters I believe it to be true.

I certify, under penalty of perjury, that the foregoing is true and correct.

Executed on _____, 19_____, at _____
_____ , California.

_____
(Name of Landlord)
Plaintiff

TO BE USED FOR RAISING RENTS

NOTICE TO CHANGE TERMS OF TENANCY

TO _____ Tenant in possession

_____

_____

    You are hereby notified that the terms of tenancy under which you occupy the above-described premises are to be changed.

    Effective _____ , 19_____ , your rent will be increased by _____ per month, from _____ per month to _____ per month, payable in advance.

    Dated this _____ day of _____ , 19_____.

_____

Owner/Manager

LEASE

This is intended to be a legally binding agreement —
Read it carefully.

Dated _____ 19_____
   at _____ , _____

1. _____ Landlord,
and _____ Tenant,
agree as follows: Landlord leases to Tenant and Tenant hires
from Landlord those premises described as: _____
_____
together with the following furniture and fixtures: _____
_____
(If list is extensive, attach hereto as exhibit "A".)
2. The term of this lease shall be _____
commencing _____ 19 _____ and terminating
_____ 19_____ .
3. If the tenant remains in the premises after the lease expires,
and the landlord accepts rent, tenancy is changed to the terms
for which the rent is paid, becoming a periodic tenancy of
month-to-month.
4. Tenant agrees to pay rent as follows: _____
_____

NOTE: The remainder of the provisions in this lease can be
      duplicated from the MONTH-TO-MONTH RENTAL
      AGREEMENT beginning with provision 3.

MONTH-TO-MONTH RENTAL AGREEMENT

This is intended to be a legally binding agreement —
Read it carefully.

Dated _____ 19_____
   at _____ , _____

1. _____ Landlord,
agrees to rent to _____ Tenant, the
premises described as: _____

together with the following furniture and fixtures: _____

(If list is extensive, attach hereto as exhibit "A".)
2. The rental shall commence on _____
19_____, and shall continue from month-to-month unless
otherwise stated here: _____

This rental may be terminated at any time by either party by giving written notice 30 days in advance, unless a longer or shorter
period of advance notice is specified here: _____ .
   Tenant agrees to pay $ _____ rent per
month on the _____ day of each month
_____ at _____
3. Tenant agrees to pay upon execution of this agreement, in addition to rent, a nonrefundable leasing charge of $ _____ .
4. Tenant agrees to pay all utilities except _____
which shall be paid for by the landlord.
5. Tenant has examined the premises and all furniture and fixtures contained therein, and accepts the same as being clean and
in good order, condition and repair, with the following exceptions: _____

6. The premises are rented for the use only as a residence for
_____ adults and _____ children.
No animal or pet except _____
shall be kept on the premises without Landlord's prior written
consent.

7. Tenant may not assign, transfer, or sublet to another person without the written consent of the Landlord.

8. Tenant shall not disturb, annoy, endanger or inconvenience other tenants of the building or neighbors, nor use the premises for any immoral or unlawful purposes, nor violate any law or ordinance, nor commit waste or nuisance upon or about the premises.

9. Tenant shall obey the Rules and Regulations for the property attached hereto.

10. Tenant shall keep the premises rented for his exclusive use in good order and condition and pay for any repairs caused by his negligence or misuse or that of his invitees. Landlord shall maintain any other parts of the property and pay for the repairs not caused by tenant's negligence or misuse or that of his invitees.

11. With tenant's permission, which shall not unreasonably be withheld, Landlord or his agent shall be permitted to enter to inspect, to make repairs, and to show the premises to prospective tenants or purchasers. In an emergency, Landlord or his agent may enter the premises without securing prior permission from tenant, but shall give tenant notice of such immediately thereafter.

12. Tenant shall neither paint nor make alterations of the property without Landlord's prior written consent.

13. If tenant abandons or vacates the premises, Landlord may at his option terminate this agreement, re-enter the premises and remove all property.

14. The prevailing party may recover from the other party his costs and attorney fees of any action brought by the other party.

15. Either party may terminate this agreement in the event of a violation of any provision of this agreement by the other party.

_____
Tenant

_____
Landlord/Manager

_____
Tenant

CARDEX (Tenant Record)

PROJ. NAME _____ # _____ PARK # _____ KEY SIGNATURE _____

Orig. Move-In Date _____

Lease Dated _____ Exp. _____

Tenant Tel. No. _____

DEPOSIT

RENT

Date Due	Date Paid	Receipt Number	Paid To Noon	Amount Paid	Security Deposit	Cleaning Fee	Key Deposit #	Base Rent	Refrigerator	Furniture	Parking	Month to Month	Additional Occupancy	Other Fireplace & Dishwasher	Air Conditioner	Utilities		Total Rent	Balance Due

BLDG. # _____ APT. _____ TYPE _____ FL. PL. _____ CLR. _____ NAME _____   Date Due _____

Glossary of Real Estate Definitions

ABANDONMENT — The voluntary relinquishment of rights of onwership of another form of interest (an easement) by failure to use the property over an extended period of time.

ABSENTEE LANDLORD — A lessor of real property (usually the owner) who does not reside on any portion of the property.

ABSTRACT OF TITLE — A summary of the conveyances, transfers, and any other data relied on as evidence of title, together with any other elements of record which may impair the title. Still in use in some states, but giving way to the use of title insurance.

ACCELERATED DEPRECIATION — Depreciation occurring at a rate faster than the normal rate. This form of depreciation is usually used for special assets for income tax purposes.

ACCELERATION CLAUSE — A clause in a mortgage or deed of trust giving the lender the right to call all monies owed him to be immediately due and payable upon the happening of a certain stated event.

ACCEPTANCE — Refers to a legal term denoting acceptance of an offer. A buyer *offers* to buy and the seller *accepts* the offer.

ACCESS RIGHT — A right to enter and exit to and from one's property.

ACCRETION — Gradual deposit of soil from a waterway onto the adjoining land. The additional land generally becomes the property of the owner of the shore or bank, except where local statutes specify otherwise.

ACCRUED DEPRECIATION — The amount of depreciation accumulated over a period of time in the accounting system for replacement of an asset.

ACKNOWLEDGEMENT — A formal declaration before an authorized official (usually a notary public) by a person who has executed a document, that he did in fact execute (sign) the document.

ACRE — A measure of land, equal to 160 sq. rods (43,560 sq. ft.). An acre is approximately 209' × 209'.

ADDENDUM — Something added. A list or other items added to a document, letter, contract, escrow instructions, etc.

ADJUSTED COST BASIS — The value on the accounting books of a taxpayer which is his original cost plus improvements less depreciation.

ADVERSE LAND USE — A use of land which causes the surrounding property to lose value, such as a truck terminal next to a residential area.

ADVERSE POSSESSION — A method of acquiring title by open and notorious possession under an evident claim or right. Specific requirements for time of possession usually vary with each state.

AFFIDAVIT — A written statement or declaration sworn to or affirmed before some official who has the authority to administer affirmation. An oath.

AGENCY AGREEMENT (LISTING) — A listing agreement between the seller of real property and a broker wherein the broker's commission is protected against a sale by other agents but not by the principal (seller). Often referred to as a nonexclusive agency listing.

AGENT — A person who is authorized to represent or act for another in business matters.

AGREEMENT OF SALE — A written contract between the buyer and the seller, where both parties are at *full* agreement on the terms and conditions of the sale.

ALIENATION — The transfer of property, or other things from one person to another.

ALIENATION CLAUSE — A clause within a loan instrument calling for a debt in its entirety upon the transfer of ownership of secured property. Also a "due-on-sale" clause.

ALL INCLUSIVE DEED OF TRUST (See Wrap-Around Mortgage).

ALLUVION — Soil deposited by accretion.

A.L.T.A. — (American Land Title Association). A group of title insurance companies which issues title insurance to lenders.

AMENITIES — Attractive or desirable improvements to property, such as a pool or view.

AMORTIZATION — The liquidation of a financial obligation using regular equal payments on an installment basis.

APPRAISAL — An estimate and opinion of value; a factual conclusion resulting from an analysis of pertinent data.

APPRECIATION — Increase in value of property from improvements or the elimination of negative factors.

APPURTENANCE — Something belonging to the land and conveyed with it, such as buildings, fixtures, rights.

ASSEMBLAGE — Process of acquiring contiguous properties into one overall parcel for a specific use or to increase value of the whole.

ASSESSED VALUE — Value placed on property by the tax assessor.

ASSESSMENT — The valuation of property for the purpose of levying a tax, or the amount of the tax levied.

ASSESSOR — One appointed to assess property for taxation.

ASSIGNMENT — A transfer or making over to another the whole of any property, real or personal, or of any estate or right therein. To assign is to transfer.

ASSIGNEE — One who receives an assignment. (Assignor — one who owns property assigned.)

ASSUMPTION OF MORTGAGE — The agreement of a buyer to assume the liability of an existing mortgage. Normally, the lender has to approve the new debtor before the existing debtor is released from the liability. (Exception to this generally with VA and FHA loans.)

ATTACHMENT — Seizure of property by court order, usually done in a pending law suit to make property available in case of judgment.

BALANCE SHEET — A financial statement which shows true condition of a business as of a particular date. Discloses assets, liabilities, and net worth.

BALLOON PAYMENT — The final installment paid at the end of the term of a note; used only when preceding installments were not sufficient to pay off the note in full.

BANKRUPTCY — Procedure of federal law to seize the property of a debtor and divide it among his creditors.

BASE AND MERIDIAN — Imaginary lines used by surveyors to find and describe the location of public or private lands.

BENCHMARK — A mark used by surveyors which is permanently fixed in the ground to denote height of that point in relation to sea level.

BENEFICIARY — The lender involved in a note and deed of trust. One entitled to the benefit of a trust.

BEQUEATH — To give or leave personal property by a will.

BILL OF SALE — An instrument used to transfer personal property.

BLANKET MORTGAGE (TRUST DEED) — A single mortgage or trust deed which covers more than one piece of real estate.

BLIGHTED AREA — A declining area where property values are affected by destructive, economic, or natural forces.

BLOCK BUSTING — A method of informing a community that people of a different race or religion are moving into the neighborhood which will cause property values to drop, thereby obtaining homes at below market values illegally.

BOARDFOOT — A unit of measuring lumber. One boardfoot is $12'' \times 12'' \times 1''$ or 144 cubic inches.

BOND — An insurance agreement by which one party is insured against loss or default by a third party. In the construction business a performance bond ensures the interested party that the contractor will complete the project. A bond can also be a method of financing debt by a government or corporation which is interest-bearing and has priority over stock in terms of security.

BOOK VALUE — The value of an asset plus improvements less depreciation.

BOOT — A term used when trading property. Boot will be the additional value given when trading properties in order to equalize values.

BOTTOM LAND — Low lying ground such as a valley. Also low land along a waterway formed by alluvial deposits.

BREACH — Violation of an obligation in a contract.

BRITISH THERMAL UNIT (BTU) — Describes the capacity of heating and cooling systems. It is the unit of heat required to raise one pound of water one degree Fahrenheit.

BROKER, REAL ESTATE — An agent licensed by the state to carry on the business of operating in real estate. He usually receives a commission for his services of bringing together buyers and sellers, owners and tenants, in exchange agreements.

BUILDING CODE — A set of stringent laws that control the construction of buildings, design, materials and other similar factors.

BUILDING LINE — A line set by law or deed restricting a certain distance from the street line, in front of which an owner cannot build on his lot. Also known as a setback line.

BUILT-INS — Items that are not movable, such as stoves, ovens, microwave ovens, dishwashers.

BUILT-UP ROOF — A form of level roof consisting of layers of roofing materials covered with fine gravel.

BUSINESS OPPORTUNITY — The sale or lease of a business and goodwill of an existing business enterprise.

BUYERS' MARKET — A market condition which occurs in real estate where more homes are for sale than there are interested buyers.

CAPITAL EXPENDITURES — Money spent by a business on improvements such as land, building, and machinery.

CAPITAL GAINS — A term used for income tax purposes which represents the gain realized from the sale of an asset less the purchase price and deductible expenses.

CAPITALIZATION — An appraising term used in determining value by considering net operating income and a percentage of reasonable return on investment.

CAPITALIZATION RATE — A percentage used by an investor to determine the value of income property through capitalization.

CASH FLOW — The owner's spendable income after operating expenses and debt service is deducted.

CAVEAT EMPTOR — A legal phrase meaning "Let the buyer beware." The buyer takes the risk when purchasing an item without the protection of warranties.

CHAIN OF TITLE — A history of conveyances and encumbrances affecting the title as far back as records are available.

CHATTEL — Personal property.

CHATTEL MORTGAGE — A mortgage on personal property.

CLIENT — One who employes the services of an attorney, real estate agent, insurance agent, etc.

CLOSING — In the sale of real estate it is the final moment when all documents are executed and recorded and the sale is complete. Also a general selling term where a sales person is attempting to sell something and the buyer agrees to purchase.

CLOSING COSTS — Incidental expenses incurred with the sale of real estate, such as appraisal fees, loan fees, termite report, etc.

CLOSING STATEMENT — A list of the final accounting of all monies of both buyer and seller prepared by an escrow agent which notes all costs each must pay at the completion of a real estate transaction.

CLOUD ON TITLE — An encumbrance on real property which affects the rights of the owner, which often keeps the title from being marketable until the "cloud" is removed.

COLLATERAL SECURITY — A separate obligation attached to another contract pledging something of value to guarantee performance of the contract.

COMMERCIAL BANK — An institution for checking accounts, loans and savings accounts and other services not found in savings and loan associations. Banks are active in installment loans on cars and boats and construction financing rather than long-term real estate financing.

COMMON AREA — That area owned in common by owners of condominiums and planned unit development homes within a subdivision.

COMMUNITY PROPERTY — Both real and personal property accumulated by a husband and wife after marriage through joint efforts of both living together.

COMPOUND INTEREST — Interest paid on the original principal and on interest accrued.

CONDEMNATION — A declaration by governing powers that a structure is unfit for use.

CONDITIONAL SALES CONTRACT — A contract for sale of property where the buyer has possession and use, but the seller retains title until the conditions of the contract have been fulfilled. Also known as a land contract.

CONDOMINIUM — A system of individual ownership of units in a multi-unit structure where each space is individually owned but each owner jointly owns the common areas and the land.

CONFORMITY, PRINCIPLE OF — An appraising term stating that uniformity throughout a certain area produces highest value.

CONSERVATOR — A court-appointed guardian.

CONSIDERATION — Anything of value given to induce someone into entering into a contract.

CONSTRUCTION LOAN — The short term-financing of improvements on real estate. Once the improvements are completed a "take-out" loan for a longer term is usually issued.

CONTINGENCY — A condition upon which a valid contract is dependent. For example: the sale of a house is contingent upon the buyer obtaining adequate financing.

CONTRACT — An agreement between two or more parties, written or oral, to do or not to do certain things.

CONTRACT OF SALE — Same as conditional sales contract or a land contract.

CONVENTIONAL LOAN — A loan made, usually on real estate, which is not backed by the Federal Government through FHA and VA.

CONVEYANCE — The transfer of the title to land from one to another.

COOPERATIVE APARTMENT — A building with two or more units wherein the right to live is acquired by the purchase of stock in a corporation which owns the property. This form of real property was a forerunner to the condominium and is not as popular due to difficulty in financing because there is no individual ownership of each unit.

CORPORATION — A legal entity having certain powers and duties of a natural person together with rights and liabilities of both, distinct and apart from those persons composing it.

COST APPROACH — A method of appraisal whereby the estimated cost of a structure is calculated less the land value and depreciation.

COUNTER OFFER — An offer in response to an offer. "A" offers to buy "B's" house for $20,000 which is listed for $22,000. "B" counter offers "A's" offer by stating that he will sell the house to "A" for $21,000. The $21,000 is a counter offer.

COVENANTS — Agreements written into deeds and other instruments stating performance or nonperformance of certain acts or noting certain uses or nonuses of the property.

C.P.M. — Certified Property Manager.

CRV (CERTIFICATE OF REASONABLE VALUE) — An appraisal of real property by the Veteran's Administration.

CUL DE SAC — A dead-end street with a turn-around included.

CURRENT ASSETS — An accounting term representing assets which can readily be converted into cash, as with short-term accounts receivable and stocks.

CURRENT LIABILITIES — Short-term debts.

D.B.A. (DOING BUSINESS AS) — A business name or identification.

DEDICATION — The donation by an owner of private property for public use.

DEED — A written instrument which when executed conveys title of real property.

DEFAULT — Failure to fulfill or discharge an obligation, or to perform any act that has been agreed to in writing.

DEFENDANT — The individual or entity against whom a civil or criminal action is brought.

DEFERRED MAINTENANCE — Normal upkeep of a property which has been postponed.

DEFERRED PAYMENTS — Payments to begin in the future.

DELIVERY — The placing of property in the possession of the grantee.

DEMISE — A lease or conveyance to another for life or years, or an estate at will.

DEMOGRAPHICS — Statistics regarding new business locations appropriate for chain stores.

DENSITY — The amount of crowding together of buildings, people, or other given things.

DEPLETION — The reduction or loss in value of an asset.

DEPOSIT RECEIPT — The form used to accept the earnest money deposit to secure the offer for the purchase of real estate.

DEPRECIATION — Loss of value of an asset brought about by age (physical deterioration), or functional and economic obsolescence. Percentage reduction of property value year-by-year for tax purposes.

DEPRESSION — That part of a business cycle where unemployment is high, and production and overall purchasing by the public is low. A severe recession.

DETERIORATION — The gradual wearing away of the building from exposure to the elements. Also referred to as physical depreciation.

DEVISE — A gift of real estate by will.

DILUVIUM — A deposit of land left by a flood.

DIMINISHING RETURNS — An economic theory that states an increase in capital or manpower will not increase production proportionately (four laborers may do less than four times the work of one laborer; and two laborers may do more than twice the work of one laborer). The return diminishes when production is proportionately less than the input.

DIRECTIONAL GROWTH — The path of development of an urban area. Used to determine where future development will be most profitable.

DIVIDED INTEREST — Different interests in the same property as in interest of the owner, lessee, or mortgagee.

DOCUMENTARY TAX STAMPS — Stamps affixed to a deed denoting the amount of transfer tax paid.

DOMICILE — The place where a person has his permanent home.

DOUBLE DECLINING METHOD OF DEPRECIATION — An accelerated method of depreciating an asset where double the amount of straight-line depreciation is used then reduced from the balance.

DOWER — The right which a wife has in her husband's estate at his death.

DOWN PAYMENT — Cash paid towards a purchase by the buyer as opposed to that amount which is financed.

EASEMENT — The legal right-of-way that permits an owner to cross another's land in order to get to his own property. Easement is appurtenant to (part of) the land and thus cannot be sold off separately and must be transferred with the title to the land of which it is a part. Other forms of rights and privileges with respect to adjacent or nearby land can be created by agreement and are also called easements to the property.

ECONOMIC LIFE — The period over which a property will yield a return on the investment.

ECONOMIC OBSOLESCENCE — Loss of useful life and desirability of a property through economic forces, such as change in zoning, changes in traffic flow, etc., rather than deterioration.

ECONOMIC RENT — The current market rental rate based on comparable rent paid for a similar unit.

EFFECTIVE AGE — The age of a structure estimated by its condition as opposed to its actual age.

EGRESS — Meaning the right to come and go across the land of another.

ELEVATION — The height above sea level. The view from the front of a structure.

EMBLEMENTS — Crops growing on the land.

EMINENT DOMAIN — The right of the Government to acquire private property for public use by condemnation. The owner must be fully compensated.

ENCROACHMENT — Trespass. The building or any improvements partly or wholly on the property of another.

ENCUMBRANCE — Anything which affects or limits the fee simple title to property, such as mortgages, trust deeds, easements or restriction of any kind. Liens are special encumbrances which make the property security for the debt.

ENTITY — An existence or being, as in a corporation or business, rather than an individual.

ENTREPRENEUR — An independent businessman taking risks for profit as opposed to a salaried employee working for someone else.

EQUITY — The value which an owner has in property over and above the liens against it. A legal term based on fairness, rather than strict interpretation of the law.

EQUITY BUILDUP — The reduction in the difference between property value and the amount of the lien as regular payments are made. The equity increases (builds up) on an amortized loan as the proportion of interest payment reduces causing the amount going toward principal to increase.

ESCALATION CLAUSE — A clause in a lease providing for an increased rent at a future time due to increased costs to lessor, as in cost of living index, tax increases, etc.

ESCHEAT — The reverting of property to the state in the absence of heirs.

ESCROW — A neutral third party who carries out the provisions of an agreement between two parties.

ESTATE — The ownership interest of a person in real property. Is also used to refer to a deceased person's property. And often used to describe a large home with spacious grounds.

ESTATE FOR YEARS — Any estate for a specific period of time. A lease.

EXCLUSIVE RIGHT TO SELL LISTING — A written contract between agent and owner where the agent has the right to collect a commission if the property is sold by anyone during the terms of agreement.

EXECUTOR — The person appointed in a will to carry out the terms of the will.

FACE VALUE — The value stated on the face of notes, mortgages, etc., without consideration of any discounting.

FAIR MARKET VALUE — That price a property will bring given that both buyer and seller are fully aware of market conditions and comparable properties.

FEASIBILITY SURVEY — A study of an area prior to development of a project in order to determine if the project will be successful or not.

FEDERAL DEPOSIT INSURANCE CORPORATION (F.D.I.C.) — The federal corporation which insures bank depositors against loss up to a specified amount (currently $40,000).

FEDERAL HOME LOAN BANK BOARD — The board which charters and regulates Federal Savings and Loan Associations and Federal Home Loan Banks.

FEDERAL HOME LOAN BANKS — Regulated by the Federal Home Loan Bank board. Currently 11 regional branches where banks, savings and loans, insurance companies or similar institutions may join the system and borrow for the purpose of making available home financing money. Its purpose is to make a permanent supply of financing available for home loans.

FEDERAL SAVINGS AND LOAN INSURANCE CORPORATION — A federal corporation which insures deposits in savings and loan associations up to a specified amount (currently $40,000).

FEE SIMPLE — Ownership of title to property without any limitation, which can be sold, left at will, or inherited.

F.H.A. (FEDERAL HOUSING ADMINISTRATION) — The federal agency which insures first mortgages on homes enabling lenders to extend more lenient terms to homeowners.

FHLMC (Freddie Mac) — Federal Home Loan Mortgage Corporation. A federal agency which purchases first mortgages from members of the Federal Reserve System and the Federal Home Loan Bank System.

FIDUCIARY — A person in a position of trust and confidence, as between principal and broker; broker as a fiduciary owes loyalty to the principal which cannot be breached under rules of agency.

FIRST MORTGAGE — A mortgage having priority over all other voluntary liens against a specific property.

FIXTURES — Items affixed to buildings or land usually in such a way that they cannot be moved without damage to themselves or the property, such as plumbing, electrical fixtures, trees, etc.

FNMA (Fannie Mae) — Federal National Mortgage Association. A private corporation which purchases first mortgages at discounts.

FORECLOSURE — Procedure where property pledged for security for a debt is sold to pay the debt in the event of default in payment and terms.

FREE AND CLEAR — A term meaning that a specific property has no liens, especially voluntary liens, against it.

FRONT FOOTAGE — The linear measurement along the front of a parcel. The portion of the parcel which fronts the street or walkway.

FUNCTIONAL OBSOLESCENCE — Loss in value due to out-of-date or poorly designed equipment while newer equipment and structures have been invented since its construction.

GNMA (Ginnie Mae) — Government National Mortgage Association. Purchases first mortgages at discounts, similar to that of FNMA.

GRADUATED LEASE — A lease which provides for rental adjustments, often based upon future determination of the cost of living index, used for the most part in long-term leases.

GRANT — To transfer an interst in real property, such as an easement.

GRANTEE — One to whom the grant is made.

GRANTOR — The one who grants the property or its rights.

GROSS INCOME — Total scheduled income from property before any expenses are deducted.

GROSS INCOME MULTIPLIER — A general appraising rule of thumb which when multiplied by the annual gross income of a property will estimate the market value.

GROSS LEASE — A lease obligating the lessor to pay all or part of the expenses incurred on leased property.

GROUND LEASE — A lease of vacant land.

GROUND RENT — Rent paid for vacant land.

HARDWOOD — Wood used for interior finish, such as oak, maple, and walnut.

HIGHEST AND BEST USE — An appraisal term for the use of land which will bring the highest economic return over a given time.

HOMEOWNERS' ASSOCIATION — An association of homeowners within a community formed to improve and maintain the quality of the community. An association formed by the developer of condominiums or planned developments.

HOMESTEAD — A declaration by the owner of a home that protects the home against judgments up to specified amounts provided by certain state laws.

HYPOTHECATE — To give a thing as security without giving up possession of it, as with mortgaging real property.

IMPOUND ACCOUNT — A trust account held for the purpose of paying taxes, insurance and other periodic expenses incurred with real property.

IMPROVEMENTS — A general term to describe buildings, roads, and utilities which have been added to raw (unimproved) land.

INCOME PROPERTY — Property which produces income.

INFLATION — The increase in an economy over its true or natural growth. Usually identified with rapidly increasing prices.

INSTALLMENT NOTE — A note that provides for regular monthly payments to be paid on the date specified in the instrument.

INSTITUTIONAL LENDERS — Banks, savings and loans or other businesses who make loans to the public during their ordinary course of business as opposed to individuals.

INSTRUMENT — A written legal document.

INTANGIBLE VALUE — The good will or well-advertised name of an established business.

INTERIM LOAN — A short-term loan usually for real estate improvements during the period of construction.

INTESTATE — A person who dies without having made a will.

INTRINSIC VALUE — The value of a thing by itself without certain aspects which will add value to some and not to others, as with a vintage Rolls Royce. It might have value to a car collector, but to anyone else it may not.

INVESTMENT — The putting up of money with the intent of making a profit.

INVOLUNTARY LIEN — A lien which attaches to property without the consent of the owner such as tax liens as opposed to voluntary liens (mortgages).

JOINT TENANCY — Joint ownership by two or more persons with right of survivorship. Upon the death of a joint tenant, his interest does not go to his heirs, but to the remaining joint tenants.

JUNIOR MORTGAGE — A mortgage which is lower in priority than a first mortgage.

LAND CONTRACT — A contract for the sale of property where the buyer has possession and use, but the seller retains title until the conditions of the contract have been fulfilled. Same as a conditional sales contract.

LAND GRANT — A gift by the Federal Government of public land.

LANDLORD — The owner of rented property.

LEASE — A contract between the owner of real property, called the lessor, and another person referred to as the lessee, covering the conditions whereby the lessee may occupy and use the property.

LEASE WITH OPTION TO PURCHASE — A lease where the lessee has the option to purchase the leased property. The terms of the purchase option must be set forth in the lease.

LEGACY — A gift of personal property by will.

LEGAL DESCRIPTION — The geographical identification of a parcel of land.

LEGATEE — One who receives personal property from a will.

LESSEE — One who contracts to rent property under a specified lease.

LESSOR — An owner who contracts into a lease with a tenant (lessee).

LEVERAGE — The use of a small amount of value to control a much larger amount of value.

LIABILITY — A term covering all types of debts and obligations.

LIEN — An encumbrance against real property for money as in taxes, mortgages, and judgments.

LIFE ESTATE — An estate in real property for the life of a person.

LIMITED PARTNERSHIP — A partnership of one or more general partners who operate the business along with one or more limited partners who contribute capital, but are only limited to the amount of money contributed.

LIQUIDATION — Disposal of property or assets, or the settlement of debts.

LIS PENDENS — A recorded legal notice showing pending litigation of real property. Anyone acquiring an interest in such property after the recording of "lis pendens" could be bound to the outcome of the litigation.

LISTING — A contract between owner and broker to sell the owner's property.

LONG-TERM CAPITAL GAIN — Gain on the sale of property that was held for at least 12 months.

M.A.I. (MEMBER APPRAISAL INSTITUTE) — A designation issued to a member of the American Institute of Real Estate Appraisers after meeting specific qualifications.

MAINTENANCE RESERVE — Money held in reserve to cover anticipated maintenance expenses.

MARKETABLE TITLE — A saleable title free of objectionable liens or encumbrances.

MARKET DATA APPROACH — An appraisal method to determine value by comparing similar properties to the subject property.

MARKET VALUE — The price a buyer will pay and a seller will accept, both being fully informed of market conditions.

MASTER PLAN — A comprehensive zoning plan to allow a city to grow in an orderly manner.

MECHANIC'S LIEN — A lien created by statute on a specific property for labor or materials contributed to an improvement on that property.

METES AND BOUNDS — A legal description used in describing boundary lines.

M.G.I.C. (MORTGAGE GUARANTY INSURANCE CORPORATION) — A private corporation which insures mortgage loans.

MINERAL RIGHTS — Ownership of the minerals beneath the ground. The owner of mineral rights doesn't necessarily own the surface land.

MORATORIUM — Temporary suspension of the enforcement of liability for a debt.

MORTGAGE — An instrument by which property is hypothecated to secure the payment of a debt.

MORTGAGE BROKER — A person who, for a fee, brings together the lender with the borrower. Also known as a loan broker.

MORTGAGEE — One who loans the money and receives the mortgage.

MORTGAGOR — One who borrows on his property and gives a mortgage as security.

MULTIPLE LISTING — A listing taken by a member of an organization of brokers, whereby all members have an opportunity to find a buyer.

NET INCOME — Gross income less operating expenses.

NET LEASE — A lease requiring tenant to pay all or part of the expenses on leased property in addition to the stipulated rent.

NET LISTING — A listing whereby agent may retain as compensation all sums received over and above a net price to the owner. Illegal in some states.

NET WORTH — Total assets less liabilities of an individual, corporation, etc.

NONEXCLUSIVE LISTING — A listing where the agent has an exclusive listing with respect to other agents; however, owner may sell the property without being liable for a commission.

NOTARY PUBLIC — One who is authorized by federal or local government to attest to authentic signatures and administer oaths.

NOTE — A written instrument acknowledging a debt and promising payment.

NOTICE TO QUIT — A notice issued by landlord to the tenant to vacate rented property, usually for nonpayment of rent or breach of contract.

OFFER — A presentation to form a contract or agreement.

OPEN LISTING — An authorization given by an owner to a real estate agent to sell his property. Open listings may be given to more than one agent without liability, and only the one who secures a buyer on satisfactory terms gets paid a commission.

OPERATING EXPENSES — Expenses relevant to income producing property, such as taxes, management, utilities, and insurance and other day-to-day costs.

OPTION — A right given, for consideration, to purchase or lease property upon stipulated terms within a specific period of time.

PERCENTAGE LEASE — A lease on property where normally a minimum specified rent is paid or a percentage of gross receipts of the lessee is paid, whichever is higher.

PERSONAL PROPERTY — Property which is not real property (real estate).

PLANNED DEVELOPMENT — Five or more individually owned lots where one or more other parcels are owned in common or there are reciprocal rights in one or more other parcels. A subdivision.

PLAT (PLAT MAP) — A map or plan of a specified parcel of land.

PLAT BOOK — A book containing plat maps of a certain area.

P.M.I. (PRIVATE MORTGAGE INSURANCE) — Insurance which covers a portion of the first mortgage allowing the lender to offer more lenient terms to a borrower.

POINT — One percent. A one-point fee is often charged by the lender to originate the loan. On FHA and VA loans, the sellers pay points to accommodate the loan.

POWER OF ATTORNEY — An instrument authorizing a person to act as the agent of the person granting it.

PRELIMINARY TITLE REPORT — The report of condition of the title prior to sale or loan transaction. Once completed a title insurance policy is issued.

PREPAYMENT PENALTY — A penalty within a note, mortgage, or deed of trust imposing a penalty if the debt is paid in full before the end of its terms.

PRIME LENDING RATE — The most favorable interest rates charged by a bank to its biggest customers.

PRINCIPAL — The employer of an agent. Also, the amount of debt, not including interest.

PRORATION OF TAXES — To divide or prorate taxes equally or proportionately to time of use.

PURCHASE AGREEMENT — An agreement between buyer and seller denoting price and terms of the sale.

PYRAMID — To build an estate by multiple acquisitions of properties utilizing the initial properties for a base for further investment.

QUITCLAIM DEED — A deed used to remove clouds on a title by relinquishing any right, title, or interest that the grantor may have.

REALTOR — A real estate broker holding membership in a real estate board affiliated with the National Association of Realtors.

REDEMPTION — The buying back of one's property after it has been lost through foreclosure. Payment of delinquent taxes after sale to the state.

R.E.I.T. (REAL ESTATE INVESTMENT TRUST) — A method of group investment with certain tax advantages, although it is governed by federal and state laws.

RENT — Consideration, usually money, for the occupancy and use of property.

REPLACEMENT COST METHOD — A method of appraisal to determine value by duplicating an exact replica.

REQUEST FOR NOTICE OF DEFAULT — A request by a lender which is recorded for notification in the case of default by a loan with priority.

RIGHT OF SURVIVORSHIP — Right to acquire the interest of a deceased joint owner. Distinguishing characteristic of joint tenancy.

RIGHT OF WAY — A privilege given by the owner of a property to give another the right to pass over his land.

RIPARIAN RIGHTS — The right of a landowner to water on, under, or adjacent to his land.

SALE-LEASEBACK — A sale of a subsequent lease from the buyer back to the seller.

SAVINGS AND LOAN ASSOCIATION — An institution which basically retains deposits from savers and lends out these deposits for home loans.

SECONDARY FINANCING — A junior loan or second in priority to a first mortgage or deed of trust.

SECURITY DEPOSIT — Money given to a landlord by the tenant to secure performance of the rental agreement.

SELLER'S MARKET — More buyers than sellers.

SEPARATE PROPERTY — Property owned by husband or wife which is not community property. Property acquired prior to marriage or by a gift, will, or inheritance.

SEVERALTY — An estate held by one person alone; although the term is misleading, it does not mean several persons own it.

SHERIFF'S DEED — Deed given by court order in connection with the sale of a property to satisfy a judgment.

SINGLE FAMILY RESIDENCE — A general term to distinguish a house from an apartment house, a condominium or a planned unit development.

SPECIAL ASSESSMENT — Legal charge against real estate by public authority to pay the cost of public improvements (sewers) by which the property is benefited.

SPECULATOR — One who buys property with the intent of selling quickly at a profit.

SPENDABLE INCOME — Net income after taxes.

SRA (SOCIETY OF REAL ESTATE APPRAISERS) — One designated SRA after receiving experience and education in the field of appraising.

STRAIGHT LINE DEPRECIATION — Reducing the value for accounting purposes over an extended period by equal increments.

STRAIGHT NOTE — A non-amortized note promising to repay a loan, signed by the debtor including the amount, when due, and interest rate.

SUBDIVISION — A division of one parcel of land into smaller lots.

SUBJECT TO MORTGAGE — When a buyer takes title to real property "subject to mortgage," he is not responsible to the holder of the note. The original maker of the note is not released form the responsibility of the note and the most the buyer can lose in foreclosure is his equity in the property.

SUBLEASE — A lease given by a lessee.

SYNDICATE — A group of investors who invest in one or more properties through a partnership, corporation, or trust.

TAKE-OUT COMMITMENT — Agreement by a lender to have available a long-term loan over a specified time once construction is completed.

TAX BASE — The assessed value which is multiplied by the tax rate to determine the amount of tax due.

TAX SALE — A sale of property, usually at auction, for non-payment of taxes assessed against it.

TENANCY IN COMMON — Ownership by two or more persons who hold an undivided interest without right of survivorship.

TENANT — The holder of real property under a rental agreement.

TENDER — An offer of money, usually in satisfaction of a claim or demand.

TENEMENTS — All rights in land which pass with the conveyance of the land. Also, commonly refers to certain groups of multiple dwellings.

TESTATOR — A person who leaves a valid will at his death.

TIGHT MONEY — A condition in the money market in which demand for the use of money exceeds the available supply.

TITLE INSURANCE — Insurance written by a title company to protect the property owner against loss if title is imperfect.

TOPOGRAPHY — Character of the surface of the land. Topography may be level, rolling, or mountainous.

TOWNSHIP — A territorial subdivision six miles long, six miles wide and containing 36 sections, each one mile square.

TRACT HOUSE — A house similar to other homes within a subdivision built by the same developer as opposed to a custom house built to owner specifications.

TRADE FIXTURES — Personal property of a business which is attached to the property, but can be removed upon the sale of the property.

TRUST DEED — An instrument which conveys legal title of a property to a trustee to be held pending fulfillment of an obligation, usually the repayment of a loan to a beneficiary (lender).

TRUSTEE — One who holds bare legal title to a property in trust for another to secure performance of an obligation.

TRUSTOR — The borrower of money secured by a deed of trust.

UNIMPROVED LAND — Land in its natural state without structures on it.

UNLAWFUL DETAINER — An action at law to evict a person or persons occupying real property unlawfully.

USURY — Interest rate on a loan in excess of that permitted by law.

VARIABLE INTEREST RATE — A fluctuating interest rate which can go up or down depending on the going market rate.

VENDEE — A purchaser or buyer.

VENDOR — A seller.

VESTED — Bestowed upon someone or secured by someone, such as title to property.

VOLUNTARY LIEN — A voluntary lien by the owner such as a mortgage, as opposed to involuntary liens (taxes).

WAIVE — To relinquish or abandon. To forego a right to enforce or require anything.

WRAP-AROUND MORTGAGE — A second mortgage which is subordinate to but includes the face value of the first mortgage.

ZONING — Act of city or county authorities specifying the types of use for which property may be used in specific areas.